# Teaching with Heart

*Inspired Teaching: Stories, Pathways,
and Strategies by
a Five-Decade Classroom Teacher
and His Former Students*

**By Ron Urick and**
***30+ of his former students***

ISBN: 9781673487275

# Dedication

This book is dedicated to all of my former students.

Wherever you are today, I thank you deeply

for enriching my life and

making my teaching career a joyful one.

Carpe Diem to all of you.


A special note of dedication to Bonnie Marlewski-

Probert who passed away in spring of 2021.

Without Bonnie's support, encouragement,

expertise, coaching, and kindness Teaching With

Heart would have not been possible.

# Table of Contents

Foreword ........................................................................ 1

Introduction ................................................................... 4

Part I: Building affect, or heart, in the classroom ................... 8

Part II: Make it interesting, make it fun ............................. 27

Part III: Let them know you believe in them ....................... 41

Part IV: Cultivate strong relationships with your students... 57

Part V: The qualities of those who inspire .......................... 72

Concluding thoughts........................................................ 97

Acknowledgements ......................................................... 99

The Teaching with Heart Team.......................................... 101

# Foreword

I remember the moment Mr. Urick noticed me as if it were yesterday. It was the second day of Accelerated Chemistry, the Fall of 1995. While standing in the hall before class, he held out his hand and asked, "What's your name again?"

"Todd Katz," I muttered, and he gripped my hand in a firm handshake.

"You're the one who liked canoeing, right?" he replied. "Tell me, have you done a fair amount of it? I love the outdoors."

Clearly, he had taken the time to read my Personal Information card, which we all filled out at the start of high school. To say I felt special was an understatement; I felt like I may have been the most important person in that school. I was a junior in high school and had never had a teacher shake my hand, or really even talk to me about my interests, let alone have a good sense of who I was by the second day of class. And at 16 years old, I had certainly shaken hands with other people, but never like this. His handshake, strengthened by what I soon learned was years of competitive bass fishing, seemed to convey a level of respect and recognition that made me think he saw me as more than just a student; that he saw me as my own person with my own likes, dislikes, opinions, and interests.

I walked into class that day thinking this was going to be a very special year. What I didn't know was that Mr. Urick would come to help lead me down a road that would inevitably allow me to follow in his footsteps as a highly respected and passionate educator.

One day in class, he said to us, "Look, I want to tell you the secret to life. It's one thing. The secret to life is to follow your passion. If you follow your passion, everything else in life will fall into place. Think about that. If you just do what you are passionate about, what you love, everything else will follow."

At 16 years old, few of us knew what we were passionate about. Keep in mind, this was a chemistry class. Not philosophy or psychology, but

1

high school chemistry. A physical science not known for promoting soulful discussions of finding lifelong fulfillment and meaning in one's personal life and career.

As a student, I was so focused and attuned to everything Mr. Urick was saying that when I think back on that moment, I understood I was being inspired. That day, his words became forever etched in my heart and have compelled me to become the type of teacher I am. He had a profound impact on the way I ended up pursuing my career and living my life.

Like Mr. Urick, I found my passion in teaching. And today, as I stand before my own freshman honors biology classes, I teach my students what it means to pursue *their* passion in a project I call "For the A."

Worth 10 percent of their quarter grade, this project is essentially the only homework my students have on a regular basis. At the start of the year, I invite them to identify something they are passionate about, interested in, or would like to learn more about. Once they have identified a topic of interest, students dedicate 15 minutes a day outside of class to it, followed by five minutes of journaling about the experience. In their journal, they reflect on the process, sharing what they would like to improve upon and what they plan to do the following day to continue growing.

After 100 minutes a week…700 to 1,000 minutes a quarter…the students have had the chance to truly delve into their passion. They learn to paint with various mediums, learn calligraphy, or practice their art, be it origami, sketching, water coloring, painting, crocheting, cooking, dance, or journaling. Some learn to master the Rubik's Cube, magic tricks, or work to improve their scales on their instruments, or how to play their favorite artist's guitar solo. My student athletes boost their vertical jump or slash milliseconds from their 50m sprint times. Meaghan focused on her downfield passing accuracy in soccer, allowing her the game-winning assist to win the city championship. Zek learned and practiced his DJ skills, creating and mixing his own beats. Three years later, he's releasing his first EP.

2

Others, like Audrey, chose writing as their passion. After dedicating her first quarter to writing poetry, her second quarter to reading and reflecting on other poets' work, and her third quarter to revising her own poems, Audrey explored self-publishing, and the result of her For the A project, titled *Between Two Open Gates*, is now available on Amazon.

Cat and Nichole tapped into their passion for the environment by connecting with an existing nonprofit and raising $1,000 for Operation Endangered Species, enough to send endangered alligators and snapping turtles to 19 different schools for care, safekeeping, and student education. Over the next three years they continued to pursue their passion (without my prompting) and by graduation, these two young women had collectively raised $48,000, with Nicole serving on the Sea World Youth Advisory Board, helping empower other students to do great things by funding their grant requests.

Equally impressive are the shyer students, whose journals tell stories of them rocking out at home as they play music they wrote themselves. The same students who would never elect to verbally participate in large group discussions are able to let go in the privacy of their own space and perform as few might ever get to witness.

What I love most about these stories is how clearly they illustrate how deeply influenced my teaching style has been by just a single sentiment Mr. Urick expressed one day in class more than 20 years ago: "If you want to be successful in life, do what you are passionate about, everything else will follow."

My entire teaching career has been crafted with that single foundational statement in mind.

*-Todd Katz, M.Ed.*
*Stevenson High School Class of '97*
*AP Environmental Science and Honors Biology teacher at Whitney M. Young Magnet High School in Chicago*
*Recipient of the Golden Apple Award, the highest teaching honor and award in Illinois*
*Passionate birder and outdoor enthusiast*

# Introduction

## *Teaching with Heart*

One of my all-time favorite movies about teaching was the 1995 film *Mr. Holland's Opus*, in which a frustrated composer named Glenn Holland (played by Richard Dreyfuss) begrudgingly embarks on what he thinks will be a temporary position as band director and music instructor in an Oregon high school. Mr. Holland's real passion is music composition; taking the teaching position is just a stopgap measure as he sees it—a short-term solution to paying the bills.

But as the film unfolds, he begins to discover the possibility and potential that lies within each of his students, and a mental shift occurs. As his outlook transforms, this "temporary position" morphs into a 180-degree career change which sees Mr. Holland, in spite of all his initial aggravations, start to love his students...and they begin to love him back.

For me, this movie beautifully captured what it means to "teach with heart" – that is, to teach with genuine passion not only for the topic at hand, but for the students you are teaching. It's a desire to know who they are as unique individuals and dedication to lighting the way for them to find their path. It means motivating and inspiring others to reach goals that might otherwise seem insurmountable.

Perhaps *Mr. Holland's Opus* spoke so clearly to me because I, like Glenn Holland, entered the teaching profession blindly. Up until my senior year at the University of Illinois-Urbana, I planned to become a mechanical engineer. Then, just a year to go before graduation, I began to experience a sense of uncertainty, a fear that mechanical engineering might not be my heart's true path to fulfillment. I had spent every summer since high school graduation working as a draftsman, surrounded by engineers. They were good, solid people, but the work environment and culture seemed to lack the softer touch I craved. I was a highly social person who loved talking and philosophizing with others, forming dynamic, heart-to-heart connections with them in the process. My intuition was nudging me into exploring other career options. Education quickly stood out as a good option. I was naturally adept at math and science, yes, but I also truly enjoyed explaining the concepts being covered in class to fellow students who felt confused or unsure. Being able to help someone grasp a tough concept felt immensely rewarding to me.

Like Mr. Holland, my entering the teaching profession felt, at first, somewhat of a dart throw. But soon I began to view it as course correction...one that ultimately ended up being my heart's true path.

Although I was trained to teach the physical sciences, I had an eye-opening diversion during my second year of teaching at Adlai E. Stevenson High School in Lincolnshire (formerly known as Prairie View), Illinois. It was the Spring of 1972, and I was asked to help develop a revolutionary interdisciplinary program for incoming freshman called "Freshman Studies." Led by 10 teachers – two each from the areas of math, science, English, social science, and physical education – along with a Freshman Studies principal, the academic year was centered around eight interdisciplinary units that transcended the traditional "reading, writing, and arithmetic" classes that at that time constituted most student schedules. In a unit called "The City," for instance, students were tasked with designing a futuristic city complete – infrastructure, governance, environmental controls, parks and recreational opportunities, transportation systems, and more. In "The Natural Environment," they studied the basics of astronomy, geology, biology, and environmental science, brought to life with exciting field trips.

Freshmen Studies students were privy to an academic experience that was years ahead of its time. I recall teaching a course called, simply, "Love" with Tom Habley, a physical education specialist with a deep interest in psychology as well as the study of human behavioral patterns. It felt radical to step outside my comfort zone of teaching pure science and jump into the worlds of affect and emotion when working with my students. The students, too, moved outside their traditional school comfort zone and responded with authenticity, feeling, artistry, creativity, caring and emotion in a way that was never previously open to them in the "normal" educational environment.

For the first time in my fledgling teaching career, I was teaching outside of my subject matter, and it felt awesome. This Freshman Studies experience opened my heart and taught me to teach with "affect," which in turn allowed me to connect with students in ways that would carry a profound, lasting impact. It ultimately shaped the way I would teach for the next four decades, a style which I, in time, began describing as Teaching with Heart.

In *Teaching with Heart*, I will attempt to offer clues about what is needed to teach passionately, inspirationally, empathically and exceptionally. It is more of an art than a science. There is no magic formula - each of us must find our own strategies and special sauce. Feel free to tweak the ingredients I spell out to fit your own teaching personality and style.

Thirty-four of my former students have graciously volunteered their time, effort, and insight to help me flesh out the meaning of Teaching with Heart. Together, they span five decades of teaching (from the 1970's through 2014) and two schools (I taught at Chicagoland Jewish High School – now known as Rochelle Zell Jewish High School – for a decade after quote-unquote retiring from Stevenson*[1]) and include a Broadway actress, a real estate attorney, an Olympic-level strength training coach, a rabbi, a dentist, an author, a child psychologist-in-training, an NBA draftee, a children's yoga and mindfulness instructor, several educators, and so much more. Drawing on their breadth and depth of experience, my students spell out who impacted them on their educational journey and offer clues to the intangibles that made this heart connection possible. In reading their narratives, perhaps you will discover ways to open doors to those "students" in your life in need of inspiration. Perhaps you, too, will be inspired.

During the late winter of 2018, I was diagnosed with prostate cancer. Being on the receiving end of a cancer diagnosis certainly punches you in the gut with a sense of your mortality and kicks off a process of reflection. *Did I live my life fully and with meaning? Did I have a positive impact on others? Will the Earth be a better place after I transition to the afterlife?* Deep questions. Profound questions.

---

[1] Throughout this book, I will refer to Adlai E. Stevenson High School as SHS, and to Chicagoland Jewish High School as CJHS.

Coming face to face with your eventual death and taking stock of how fully you have lived has a way of pushing you toward any goals lingering on your To Do list. The idea to author this book had been sparked long before my diagnosis. But life got in the way. I was teaching. Our son, Nick, was still young and I was highly involved with his schooling, sports, and musical activities. As a family, we traveled often – Disney World and annual hiking trips at more than a dozen national parks around the country. The book idea fell on the back burner.

Then, I heard the words, "You have cancer."

Fortunately, my tumor proved to be a very slow-growing cancer often associated with the natural aging process. In fact, I was told my cancer required no treatment, but could instead be managed via careful monitoring by my physician. This was wonderfully relieving news for my family and me, to say the least. But nevertheless, I had felt the tap on the shoulder to get going on the goals in life I had yet to accomplish.

Writing this book is my "Opus" to the educational community, and to you.

*-Ron Urick, September 2019*

# Part I

## *Building affect, or heart, in the classroom*

The first few days of the school year are critical in building what I call "heart connections" with students. Over the years, as my students entered my classroom for the first time, I would ask them to choose a seat and immediately drew up a seating chart. My homework that night: To memorize every chart, so I could call on each of them by name by the following day.

On Day One of a new school year, I also played what I called The Standup Game. It begins with all students sitting down. Then you start to give the class a series of "Stand up if..." directives: "Stand up if you are an only child" or "Stand up if you play a musical instrument." After each one, pause for a few moments to ask the newly standing students for some more details: "Tell us a bit about what it was like being an only child" or "What instrument? How long have you played?"

Some other good *Stand Up*s to try:

*"Stand up if you can speak fluently in two or more languages."* ("Which languages? What prompted you to learn them?")

*"Stand up if you have ever had a near-death experience."* ("Can you tell us about it?")

*"Stand up if you have successfully overcome a fear."* ("Can you tell us about it?")

*"Stand up if you play a sport."* ("What sport"?)

You get the idea. Questions should be geared around the age and maturity of the students in your classroom, but other than that, they are limited only by your creativity and judgement.

As we played Stand Up on Day One, I'd have my seating chart in front of me and would start adding a few key words under each student's

8

name. More Night One homework for me: memorize one personal tidbit about each student.

For *their* homework that first night, I had them complete a Student Profile, a sheet I had created with numerous questions designed to encourage them to open up and share some of themselves with me.

*"Tell me about the personal accomplishment of which you are most proud, and why."*

*"Where do you see yourself in 10 years?"*

*"If you won $10 million in the lottery, what would you do with the money?"*

*"Name an individual you deeply respect and tell me why."*

On Day Two, I would collect all the Student Profile sheets, then begin class by addressing each student by name along with one fact about them, culled from Stand Up the day prior. They would be impressed! Indeed, this is precisely why I knew that Todd Katz (the author of this book's Foreword) loved canoeing when we shook hands on the second day, just before the period bell rang.

For my homework on Night Two, I pored over the Student Profiles. On occasion, I read them out loud to my wife or son, which helped cement each student's attributes in my mind. I truly wanted to get to know every one of my students on a personal level before diving into reaction rates and states of matter. This is so critical in building authentic "heart" connections to your students.

## Kick off your school year with a bang

I was also never that anxious to jump into teaching "content" without first wowing my students with some exciting chemical demonstrations, so the very first minute of class, before we embarked on Stand Up, I performed my "invisible ink" trick.

Using phenolphthalein, a colorless organic liquid compound, I would write a secret message on my paper-covered whiteboard. Then I'd grab a spray bottle filled with an ammonia solution, knowing that when phenolphthalein encounters a base, like ammonia, it turns vibrant pink. As I sprayed the board, the message "Welcome to Mr. U's Chemistry Class!!" emerged. This magic trick never failed to energize the students.

You don't have to be a chemistry instructor to employ your own WOW-worthy Day One maneuver. And it needn't be showy. It just needs to spark curiosity and churn up a bit of excitement to gain students' attention, giving them a tiny taste of the secret magic that resides in the topic you yourself know and love so well. A physics teacher could challenge the class to prove that the Earth isn't flat, perhaps dividing them into teams for brainstorming and then have them each present their cases, pitting one team against the other. Psychologist Sarah Rose Cavanagh, Ph.D., a tenured associate professor at Assumption College in Worcester, Massachusetts, and author of *The Spark of Learning: Energizing the College Classroom with the Science of Emotion,* passes out sheets of paper on the first day and asks her students to answer the question, "What is one weird thing your brain does?" (Stand-out responses over the years have included psychic experiences; a student who claimed to be able to remember every license plate ever seen; and have even revealed a few synesthetes, which are individuals who cross-perceive sensory input, like experiencing music as color or "tasting" words!)[i]

In the inspirational film *Dead Poet's Society*, Robin Williams plays an unorthodox English teacher at an elite boys' boarding school. On the first day of class, he invites his students to look at the photographs of young men – alumni – hanging on the wall. These are photos they've all passed by countless times before, but most likely have never bother to notice. "They're not that different from you, are they?" Williams' Mr. Keating asks. "Did they wait until it was too late to make from their lives even one iota of what they were capable? Because, you see, gentlemen, these boys are now fertilizing daffodils. But, if you listen real close, you can hear them whisper their legacy to you. Go ahead, lean in. Listen....you hear it?" Then Mr. Keating himself whispers, "*Carpe Diem. Seize the day, boys. Make your lives extraordinary.*"

*Carpe Diem* is one of the phrases I have chosen to live my own life by – I often use it when signing off of emails – and it's a theme I very intentionally wove throughout my classes. For me, kicking off each semester with a secret phenolphthalein message was my first, somewhat undercover attempt at communicating this zeal for life. I believe in living life with passion and have made it a point to pursue my interests with that passion, whether it's when teaching my students, loving my family, or enjoying fishing, hiking and my other beloved outdoor pursuits. And I consistently made a point of conveying this sentiment to my students, both explicitly and implicitly, through my excitement for our day's activities.

Remember that building affective connections with your students is a two-way street. You requested a personal profile from each of your students. Now be sure to tell your students about *you*—your passions and interests; your family. Tell them what personal accomplishments *you* are proud of and what *you* would do if you won $10 million in the lottery. They need to know you as well as you know them.

## *Let the students help set the rules*

*"There is always time to do things that really matter."* —Peter Block

The way you start a school year is critical. Your first few days with students in a class will set the tone of the entire school year.

In my high school chemistry class, I chose to run things like a democracy rather than a dictatorship. Instead of handing my students a sheet that spelled out the existing "Rules and Expectations," I asked them to generate their own list. We would spend one of the first days of the semester breaking into groups to brainstorm the ingredients of a successful class. "Imagine you are starting a business," I would say, "and your overarching goal is to hire employees who will help your company succeed. What qualities would you look for in those employees?" Without exception, the following always showed up on my classes' lists, year after year:

* Willingness to work hard

* Excellent communication skills

* Mutual respect

These tenets served as the foundation for our Class Rules. Students were expected to behave in a way that honored these principles at all times. Their dedication to this was factored into their grades. For instance, I made it very clear to students that for anyone on the cusp of a certain grade, my subjective assessment of how hard they worked both inside and outside of class would determine whether that cusp grade would get a boost upward or a boost downward.

By guiding your students and empowering them to create their own list of class bylaws, you're actually teaching them a crucial life skill. You're helping them identify the kind of person they one day aspire to be; the type of partner they want to be (and be with); and the treatment they believe they deserve from others. Ask any NFL football player or accomplished concert pianist or couple in a 50-year-plus happy marriage if tenets like hard work, communication, and mutual respect played a role...I think you know what the answer will be. With this trifecta in place, you put yourself in an excellent position to succeed – in academics, at work, in friendships and romantic relationships, in parenting, and more.

## *Host guest teachers*

*"And, in the end/The love you take/Is equal to the love you make."—* Paul McCartney

One of the most powerful things you can do in your classroom is invite a former student back to teach your current classes. Hosting a guest teacher of this caliber is like offering your current students a career crystal ball. They can't help but picture themselves up there at the front of the class, having graduated high school and immersed in some wonderfully cool new world of studies. Because the guest teacher has been in their exact shoes, your students will feel more at ease, which allows them to better grasp the information being imparted. These guest speakers bring a freshness to your classroom --a change of pace.

And they illustrate that yes, the students can be successful and perhaps one day return to their former high school to do the same.

I recall asking a past student named Eileen Li (now Eileen Rose) to return to SHS to teach my accelerated chemistry classes at SHS when she was a Senior at Northwestern University majoring in biochemistry. The year was 2000. Just a few years prior, she had been sitting in my own class, a passionate chemistry student who earned the highest grade on the June final exam, thus winning my guided fishing trip give away (more on this later.)

As a guest teacher, Eileen chose to lead a lab session during which students would create luminol, the material that allows male fireflies to produce the glowing light that attracts their mates. As Eileen deftly took control of the class, I sat back and became an observer, proudly watching my former chemistry student dazzle my current ones.

It was slightly surreal to watch this accomplished young lady, who had been a sophomore student in my high school chemistry class and was now so obviously passionate about teaching a slice of chemistry to my current students. What great joy! The inspiration had gone full circle.

Another notable former student who made multiple visits to my classes was Dr. Rohen Jobanputra, who at the time of his visits was a highly regarded orthopedic surgeon in the Chicagoland area. I'd had the pleasure of teaching Dr. Ro when he was a 16-year-old sophomore student in my honors chemistry class at SHS. Before Dr. Rohan's first guest teacher visit, he told me that he was planning to bring with him a videotape of a knee replacement surgery he had performed. Of course I asked, "Will the video be bloody and gruesome?" To be honest, I wasn't too concerned about my students' ability to handle it, but I want to make sure that *I* wouldn't pass out!

Dr. Ro obliged by bringing in a video of him operating on the arthritic big toe joint of an avid runner—a little gruesome to view, but tolerable for those with weaker stomachs. Standing before my class, Dr. Ro would talk frankly about the realities of medical school and preparing to enter the medical profession. He told the students he had always been a "tool guy"—he loved drills, saws, and screws, and now those same tools were an integral part of his surgeries. He had a great sense of humor and always introduced some levity into his presentations. (This is the same person who, as my student, once asked if he could "sample" the fermented ethanol – i.e. drinking alcohol – we had created in class from a combination of water, yeast, and molasses. My response was, "If you put a drop on your tongue, I didn't see it happen." These were the 1980's and things were looser.) My kids loved Dr. Ro. So did I. Again, the inspiration had come full circle.

(Dr. Ro passed away in July of 2019 at age 53 after a short battle with a highly aggressive cancer. He was a deeply grateful man and thanked me every time we spoke about steering him in the right career direction, and for being tough on him as a student in my class. I spoke at his funeral. We definitely had a genuine heart connection. I miss him deeply.)

Parents are also an outstanding resource. More often than not, you can find a parent willing to share his or her course-relevant passion with your current classes. I once had a student whose father was a Quaker Oats flavor chemist responsible for designing esters, which are the flavoring and scenting compounds used to imbue certain foods and drinks with their characteristic odor and taste. This parent arrived in class with a suitcase full of esters in tiny vials: Banana, coffee, licorice, watermelon, wintergreen, lemon, strawberry, and more. He embarked on an engaging experiment by blindfolding one of my students and asking him to come to the front of the class, guided by another student. At the demonstration table, the chemist took out a small bag of buttered popcorn and placed it at one end of the demo table. At the other end, he had placed a piece of tissue he had sprayed with buttered popcorn ester. He guided the blindfolded student to each end of the table and asked him to identify the real popcorn by smell alone. In nearly every class, the blindfolded student mistook the ester-sprinkled tissue for the real thing. Great fun!

Another notable parent was an elementary particle physicist at the Fermi Lab in Batavia, Illinois. During our unit on atomic structure, he joined us to talk about the elusive "Higgs boson," the so-called "God particle" thought to be responsible for all mass in the universe. The particle has proved extraordinarily hard to detect, but physicists believe that it is crucial for Unification of the Four Forces in Nature: gravity, electromagnetism, the weak nuclear force, and the strong nuclear force. It's heady stuff – particle physics is so mysterious and obscure that it's almost like a fantasy. My students were captivated and so was I.

Take advantage of your entire learning community and all the resources within it. Guest instructors will be flattered by the invitation, and the students will benefit tremendously.

# STUDENT REFLECTIONS

*Leslie (Goldman) Alter*
*SHS '94*

It all started with her spider tattoo.

Ms. Maxwell taught World Masterpieces at SHS, where she was charged with leading us through an exploration of classics such as Mary Shelley's *Frankenstein* and *Things Fall Apart* by Chinua Achebe. I was a strong student with a love of writing, but had never thought to pursue it as a career. In grade school, I'd tinkered with fiction, penning silly essays that my middle school teachers let me read aloud to the class, but a combination of passionate interest in health, awe for the human body, and a touch of hypochondria had led me to choose medicine as my future profession.

Similarly, my family had raised me to believe that women and men were equal – my maternal grandparents in particular offered me my first exposure to feminism (without actually calling it that) by role modeling what undying respect and mutual support look like in a relationship – but I had never considered calling myself a feminist. Every month, I devoured my beloved *Sassy* magazine (I'm dating myself!) filled with profiles of kickass feminist girls changing the world, but they remained somewhat fictionalized to me. I was a high school senior, convinced that boyfriends and popularity went hand-in-hand with happiness.

Then along came Ms. Maxwell. She had dark wavy hair and enormous blue eyes and wore black and had a tattoo of a spider on her ankle. She told us that she had gotten it during graduate school to commemorate her introduction to – and ultimately, her full immersion in – feminism and women's literature. The spider, she explained, represents the methods often used by women when writing and getting our voices heard – perhaps because, historically-speaking, our storytelling has tended to be more "web-like" versus linear, but also because for centuries, women weren't permitted to publish their writing, so we had to "weave" our stories into the popular narrative.

Ms. Maxwell ("My first name's Elizabeth, but my friends call me Betsy," she told us) used classic books to prompt us to examine our own worldviews. She showed so much enthusiasm when we answered questions or offered up opinions that we could *feel* how much she believed in us. There was an almost magical ambiance in her class, where students from all different cliques seemed to mingle effortlessly. She was the first person to explicitly encourage me to question gender norms. And because there were male students as well as female in our class, it made it feel safer, in a way, to do so, as she was simultaneously challenging *them* to rethink gender roles as well.

I'm now a magazine writer myself, focusing on women's health, nutrition, psychology, parenting, and the like. I also love interviewing women who are doing awe-inspiring things and sharing their stories with the world, like the former realtor who started a holistic homeless shelter for women and children in Miami, or the first female U.S. soldier to lose a limb in Iraq who is now an U.S. Paralympic medalist and coaches others who have lost limbs to compete. I'm living my *Sassy* dream, in large part because of this teacher.

Ms. Maxwell and I reconnected about seven years ago and went out for dinner, re-bonding over sauvignon blanc and seafood risotto. She always Likes or comments on my posts featuring my writing, giving me the same buzz I might get if Oprah herself were hitting the thumbs up button. Her Facebook page shows the same Ms. Maxwell I knew back in 1994: in a pink hat at the Women's March with a "Stay Nasty" poster; dressed up as Hester Prynne for Halloween, a big scarlet A emblazoned on her chest (and her SHS science teacher husband by her side as a priest); beaming in photos alongside her children, as well as her students.

Ms. Maxwell taught us that women don't need to dress or act a certain way just to be considered smart or powerful or attractive. She emboldened us to question and to push. Decades before the #MeToo movement, I had this teacher, so full of heart and passion, who not only talked the talk, but walked the walk... that spider peeking out with every step.

*Leslie (Goldman) Alter earned a Bachelor of Science degree in nutritional science from the University of Wisconsin-Madison and a Master's degree in Public Health from the University of Illinois-Chicago. She is a freelance magazine journalist whose work regularly appears in publications such as* O: The Oprah Magazine; Real Simple, Women's Health, Parents, Prevention, *and more. Leslie has authored, co-authored, and ghost written several books and frequently appears on national and local news shows as a guest expert on women's issues. She lives in Chicago with her husband, Dan, and two daughters.*

*Tyler Uteg*
*SHS '02*

My first memory of a teacher connecting with me on a personal level dates back to Mrs. Miller's third grade English class at Laura B. Sprague school in Lincolnshire, Illinois. She had us read *Where the Red Fern Grows*, a classic book about a young boy who dreams of owning coonhound hunting dogs. Billy saves up his money to buy two pups, Old Dan and Little Ann. It's a touching story of adventure, enduring friendship, and loyalty.

This book, and Mrs. Miller, started me on a path toward my lifelong love of the outdoors. I still remember my discussions with her, bonding over our love for the storyline. The book got me outside and drove me to be inquisitive about nature. I also remember wanting to get coonhounds for myself, even though I lived in the suburbs of Chicago and not in the Ozarks, as Billy did.

In response to my interest, Mrs. Miller did something so unexpected: she invited me out to dinner with her husband to discuss the book more in depth. Who takes a third grader to dinner, outside of school hours, simply because that student is passionate about a book?! Mrs. Miller did, and I hope she knows how that kindled a fire in me at a very young age.

Then there was Mr. Mapes, who taught my sixth grade science class at Daniel Wright Jr. High School in Lincolnshire, Illinois. In his class, we frequently discussed our shared love for fishing, one of my outdoor passions that had been kindled by Mrs. Miller. At some point during my time in Mr. Mapes' class, he mentioned that he was selling a 16-foot aluminum jonboat. I was only 11 years old, but I pounced at the idea of buying it and being able make my own memories in it. Lucky for me, Mr. Mapes had priced the boat at a very reasonable $100, which my parents gifted to me as a birthday present.

I still remember Mr. Mapes bringing it to my parents' house on top of his old VW bus, and the joy it brought me to see it in person. I named it the "Fat Bass 1," and still have the original drawing outlining my grand plans I had for the vessel. It was this interaction, and Mr.

Mapes' heartfelt gesture, that continued to drive me toward my addiction for all things fishing. Many years, and several seaworthy boats later, I still look back fondly at this time in my life and how a teacher went above and beyond to encourage a passion in a random student, well outside the bounds of traditional education. I can honestly say that seemingly small thing helped shape me into the person I am today, and I won't ever forget it.

In between sixth grade and high school, it took a while before I had a teacher who I truly felt went above and beyond to "teach with heart." It may sound like a plant, given he's the author of this book, but that teacher was Mr. Urick. At that point in my life, I was not the best student, and certainly didn't want to be in school every day when there were fish to be caught. But Mr. Urick's ability to weave his fishing stories and successes into his curriculum connected with me. His class felt more like "fun" than "academics," even though we were clearly learning the ins and outs of high school chemistry. I'll never forget Bass-o-rama, where we had to flip a bait into a cup from across the room. I wanted so badly to win, but fell short as my fishing skills were not then what they are today. Still, the fact that my teacher had a passion for fishing that seemed to rival my own…that stuck with me.

One final teacher I'm honored to mention is my father, Don, who was our district school board president for nearly a decade. My father founded, built, and managed a home lighting store called The Lamp Shader for 42 years. Growing up, I spent a great deal of time with both of my parents at the store, where I learned how to do things like create original lamps for customers using treasured, sentimental objects, like a beloved vase. My dad showed me that it was possible to create a business, be active in the community, have a family, *and* be that rare person who actually loves what they do for a living.

The teachers who impacted and inspired me the most were the ones who didn't just show up and teach the same curriculum year after year, but instead would adjust, connect, and really breathe life into the classroom, making kids feel excited to be there. I've also always found the best teachers are those who are willing and able to work with each student at an individual level without giving up. They have the ability to connect on a personal level beyond the classroom, to impart valuable lessons that won't be found in any textbook. They might not have realized it at the time, but these teachers changed my direction in life and helped drive me to become the person I am today in seemingly small, but truly profound, ways.

*Tyler Uteg earned his undergraduate degree in communications, along with a minor in entrepreneurship, from the University of Iowa, and is a business operations professional based in Chicago, where he lives with his wife, Elyse. When he's not at his day job, you can find Tyler on his bass boat fishing the many lakes in and around Wisconsin.*

*Eileen (Li) Rose*
*SHS '96*

I grew up in Beijing and came to the U.S. the summer I turned 13 years old. My mother had moved here four years earlier to pave the way for a better life for our family. During those four years, many people went the extra mile to make sure I didn't feel alone.

Mrs. Zhang, my fourth grade English teacher in Beijing, was one of them. She taught me the importance of self-respect and independence, while acting as a sort of surrogate mother for me while my mom was in the U.S.. Mrs. Zhang carried herself with amazing posture, seeming to stand taller than her peers. She weaved crucial life lessons into her curriculum. Lessons like:

-Just because a person is loud doesn't mean he or she is correct, and just because a person is quiet doesn't mean he or she is weak.

-Don't be afraid to ask questions or voice your opinion.

-Girl or boy, small or tall, I can be as strong as anyone.

I brought these lessons with me when I moved to the U.S. There, Mrs. Kueck became my ESL (English as a Second Language) teacher. She was the mother of one of my classmates, and was the first teacher to ever invite me into her home, an experience I'll never forget. Mrs. Kueck had a piano in her house. Growing up in China, we'd had a piano in our home, but I had never learned to play. Mrs. Kueck told me that she herself did not learn to play until later in life. She promised me that if I put my mind to it, I could accomplish anything I wanted, whether that was learning to play piano or mastering English.

When you teach with heart, you make teaching personal. You assure your students that mistakes are not to be feared. You welcome them into your heart. You become a role model. The rewards are rarely immediate, but trust that your students feel it, we pay it forward, and we are forever grateful

*Eileen (Li) Rose graduated with a Bachelor of Arts degree in biochemistry and cell biology from Northwestern University in Evanston, Illinois. She currently works as a senior scientist at a startup biotech company in the San Francisco Bay Area and lives with her husband and mother-in-law.*

*Rabbi Elli Cohn*
*CJHS '09*

Throughout my 21 years as a student, the teachers who exhibited patience, a sense of calm, an openness to student ideas, an encouraging demeanor, and genuine excitement about the course or topic always inspired me the most. However, the two qualities that I believe had the most profound impact on me were passion and love. The teachers who demonstrated passion about their courses helped me learn exponentially more than the teachers who didn't display their passion as sincerely…or at all.

Similarly, the teachers who taught with heart, who decided that they loved each and every student before they even got to know them – those are the teachers who have stuck with me most. The teachers who taught with love didn't try to "fix" students who perhaps didn't connect with the topic at hand, or who needed extra help. They considered and reflected on each student individually and asked, "How can I help this particular student succeed?"

In high school, I often met with teachers to discuss a difficult homework assignment or challenging essay prompt. For the teachers who truly taught with heart, I left their offices with more than just a solved problem or a more refined thesis statement. Something else happened during these encounters that I believe was even more valuable. The best teachers were part of a collective effort to help me grow into the best version of myself. They challenged me to ask myself: "What are my values?"…"How do I want to carry myself in this world?"…"Who am I becoming?"…"What do I love to do?"

It's not that they directly asked these questions, or taught a class called "How to Become the Best Version of Yourself." Rather, they used real pastoral care to guide me as I navigated these questions in real time, fostering a dynamic that allowed to me to feel comfortable trying to figure these things out. They held space for me, so I could experiment with asking questions and finding my answers. They helped me see that what would carry me further in life was not a straight-A report card or stellar ACT score, but the quality of my character; my instinct

23

and desire to help others; and a lifelong commitment to growing and evolving.

This helped me navigate the growing pains that come along with the process of self-discovery. For many high school students, this is a time when we start identifying our values, and perhaps realizing that what drives us in the world may be different than what we've learned at home. This can be challenging to go through – learning to own your identity, to be your own person separate and distinct from your parents and maybe even from your friends. Self-discovery is powerful and liberating, but also scary and intimidating. The best teachers I had in high school bolstered me as I embarked on this right-of-passage process. They lifted me up. The experience informed my decision to become a rabbi and high school teacher myself, so that I could try to touch the hearts of students in the same way that my own teachers touched mine. If I achieve even a small fraction of the impact my teachers had on me, I will have succeeded.

*Rabbi Elli Cohn earned her Bachelor of Arts in religion studies from Muhlenberg College in Allentown, Pennsylvania, before embarking on her rabbinical training at The Jewish Theological Seminary in New York City in 2013. She was ordained as a rabbi in 2018 and currently teaches Jewish Studies at Gann Academy, a pluralistic Jewish high school in Waltham, Massachusetts.*

*Ellen Saharack Singer*
*SHS '87*

Throughout my time in school, I connected with many teachers on a personal level, which likely led to my choosing a career in education. But the teacher who stands out most in my mind is Joan Ackerman-Zimny, my seventh and eighth grade Advisory teacher.

At our middle school, lunch was followed by a 30-minute period called "Advisory," which was devoted to addressing social-emotional issues. It featured lots of activities based on team-building skills, with time built in to learn, discuss, and practice study skills. Advisory was a mix of seventh and eighth grade students – one of the few times these grades interacted throughout the school day.

I always looked forward to Advisory. Our teacher, Joan Ackerman-Zimny, showed genuine concern for each of us, taking the time to learn about everyone not just as students, but as human beings. She spent time with us, engaging in deep, meaningful conversations. Joan introduced fun games that brought together students who did not have a lot in common, breaking down grade and clique barriers and giving us a sense of community. Joan taught us that everyone is worthy, that every individual has something to bring to the table, and instilled in us the importance of listening and having empathy.

I can tell you that most of my friends did not feel this way about their advisory leader, many of whom seemed to be doing just the bare minimum – what they were "supposed" to do. Many of my peers found Advisory boring and a waste of time. Our Advisory was different.

Joan not only took the time to develop strong relationships with us, but she encouraged us to cultivate strong relationships with one another, to step outside our comfort zones and make new friends with students who we'd known for years, but never had the opportunity to bond with. Her commitment and passion for her students helped me build my confidence and spread my wings.

25

*Ellen Saharack Singer is chair of the fine arts department at Rochelle Zell Jewish High School in Deerfield, Illinois, as well as a vocal music teacher. She has also served as director of the SHS Madrigal Choir since 1995. Ellen earned her Bachelor of Science degree in music education from the University of Illinois and her Master of Music degree from DePaul University. She has taught general music and choir to students of all grade levels in several public school districts. Ellen is the mother of 20-year-old triplet boys, whom she lives with in Buffalo Grove, Illinois.*

# Part II

## Make it interesting, make it fun

*"Nothing great is ever achieved without enthusiasm."*
— Emerson

Several decades ago, I invented a game called "Chemistry Baseball," which blended the competitive elements of baseball with the varying-levels-of-difficulty quiz components of *Jeopardy*. It can easily be adapted to any subject though. All you need is a whiteboard or chalkboard and a set of index cards marked with questions or problems designed to reflect the topic or unit currently being studied. Make sure you have questions of varying levels of difficulty, classified as Single, Double, Triple or Home Run (Home Run being the hardest.)

Before class begins, use colored dry-erase markers or chalk to draw a baseball diamond on the board, marking first base, second base, third base, and home plate. Once everyone is seated, divide the class into two teams, flipping a coin to decide which team will begin at bat and which will be the visiting team. When the Visiting team begins batting, the first player at bat can request a single, double, triple or home run question. If the question is answered correctly in a reasonable about of time (you decide what is reasonable), put the student's initials alongside the appropriate base. An incorrect answer results in an Out.

My students loved playing Chemistry Baseball – even the kids who weren't into sports *at all*. It was a novel way to review material in a fun, low-stress manner, plus it promoted team-work and communication.

## The science behind the fun

Injecting joy into class is a fundamental principle of Teaching with Heart, and it turns out that neuroscience research backs it up.

Neurologist-turned-middle school teacher Judy Willis, M.D., M.Ed., has written extensively about strategies to fuel student learning,

27

include a model she calls R.A.D. Lessons in the Classroom. The acronym's three letters each stand for a region or process of the neural system that becomes activated when learning is *fun*:

1.  When information is presented in a novel way, it promotes the transmission of that new information through the **R**eticular Activating System, a network of nerve pathways in the brain that filters out frivolous or unnecessary data, ensuring that the most important things a person sees and hears become properly stored. It's like an automatic filter, as well as a focus-enhancer. Have you ever had the experience of a friend telling you about something she heard in the news that you hadn't, and then suddenly, it seems like you can't stop reading about it or hearing about it?[ii] That's your Reticular Activating System at work. In her book, *Research-Based Strategies to Ignite Student Learning: Insights from a Neurologist and Classroom Teacher,* Dr. Willis writes, "Gaining and keeping student's attention will promote information passage from simple momentary awareness to working memory and then to stored long-term memory banks…Connected minds stay focused." [iii]

2.  A low-stress, intimidation-free classroom environment helps to move data through the **A**mygdala, a region of the brain that lights up when a person feels scared or threatened. In a stressful learning environment, the amygdala can become over-activated, causing a student to feel anxious and discouraged. In this state, new information cannot pass through to become stored.[iv]

    But! When stress is low and enjoyment levels are high, the amygdala remains calm…and information can get through. An entertaining game like Chemistry Baseball disguises learning as recreation, keeping stress low and helping any information being reviewed to really get cemented in the brain.

3.  When a classroom activity feels fun, the brain releases **D**opamine, a feel-good neurotransmitter that stimulates the brain's memory centers and triggers the release of a chemical called acetylcholine, which boosts attention even more.[v]

There you have it: Make learning interesting, make learning fun. Make it **R.A.D**. Do everything in your power to make your class come alive.

Here's another example: In chemistry, we study a concept called "the mole and stoichiometry," which relates to quantitative relationships in chemical reactions. It's all about proportionality and basic math, and can be rather dry, and I wanted to find a way to spice the unit up. So, towards the end of our stoichiometry unit, I would offer an extra credit assignment in which students could build "moles"—animal moles, that is; a pun on the chemical concept. Any participating student would receive a pattern to define the relative size of his or her mole. It was then up to them to decide whatever material they would use to construct their mole—usually fabric, though the rare mole was erected out of clay, aluminum foil, newspaper or papier mâché. This was all done outside of class hours.

Over the decades, nearly all of my students elected to take on the project, which culminated in the Annual Mole Award Day (a.k.a. "The Acad-Mole-ee Awards,") during which the most clever, creative, funny, and well-constructed mole was named. The event was advertised throughout the school, with faculty and former students serving as "mole judges" for the day. The mole receiving the most votes was named Celebrity Mole for that school year. Some past winners and notable submissions have included "The Hunchback of Molar Dame," "Mole of America," "Barrack Mole-Bama," "Guac-a-Moley," "Whack-a-Mole", "A Mole-in-One," "Osama Mole-Laden," "Wooly Mole-moth," "Moleby Dick," "No 'Mole' Garciaparra," "The Mole-er-cyclist," and "Kodak Molement." One year, a cheeky student handed me a mole made of nothing – it was just empty air. He called it "The Invisa-Mole." I responded by saying he would be awarded "invisa-points." Then, there was the young man who turned in "Pam-mole-Ahh Anderson," a topless mole which I had to veto for obvious reasons. Our class enjoyed lots of hearty laughs over that one, though.

## *Find the right niche*

Christopher Emdin, PhD, creator of the #HipHopEd social media movement, uses music to reach students. His nonprofit organization assists teachers, school leaders, and policymakers in developing and implementing hip hop-based interventions as a means of fostering interest among urban youth in the STEM (Science, Technology, Engineering, and Math) fields. For example, Dr. Emdin's Science Genius initiative focuses on "utilizing the power of hip-hop music and culture to introduce youth to the wonder and beauty of science. The core message of the initiative is to meet urban youth who are traditionally disengaged in science classrooms on their cultural turf, and provide them with the opportunity to express the same passion they have for hip-hop culture for science."[vi]

When Brooklyn Preparatory High School began offering its Science Genius B.A.T.T.L.E.S. (Bringing Attention to Transforming, Teaching, and Learning Science) Program with the help of #HipHopEd, it culminated in a tournament at the Jacob Javits Center in New York, where students competed in science-themed rap battles. Sample lyrics by then-senior Jaiyer Millington:

*Look! The cause of your demise, I can see it 'cause I got the vision/Hit your shoulders several times, break the scapula humerus connection/And I subtract your femur from your hamstring, now your legs is missing/Add me to the equation, it's a smooth operation!*[vii]

As a result of #HipHopEd, educators have reported improved attendance, higher test scores, and more enthusiastic attitudes towards science content among engaged students. Dr. Emdin, who serves as Director of the Science Education program and Associate Director of the Institute for Urban and Minority Education at Columbia University's Teachers College in New York City, has written his own opus, the *New York Times* bestseller *For White Folks Who Teach in the Hood... and the Rest of Y'all Too: Reality Pedagogy and Urban Education*. He recognizes the value in knowing your audience and tailoring your teaching style to them, rather than trying to stuff your teaching lessons into some generic mold. Make it interesting, make it fun!

# Bass-o-Rama

The day before winter break was one of my favorite days of the school year. I never scheduled a test, quiz, or anything too academic on this day. Instead, it was a day to share my passion for bass fishing with my students. By this point, they all knew how momentous a role fishing played in my life. Now, winter break was upon us which meant just one thing: It was time to celebrate Bass-o-Rama Day.

Students loved the day as much as I did. Your students need to know YOU as well as you know them. My fishing addiction was much more than a serious hobby—it was a second career for me. I have competitively fished for decades and have been very successful in these competitions— winning cash along with a fully rigged Ranger bass boat, trailer, and outboard motor over the years. I am a licensed fishing guide and run a business called "On the Water Bass Clinic," an instructional service where I teach the finer points of bass fishing to clients. While teaching, I annually awarded a free guided fishing day to the high finishers on my June Final Exam. Since I taught both honors chemistry as well as college prep chemistry, there were two winners every year. The kids loved it and Mr. Urick's end-of-the-year fishing trip became a coveted prize at SHS. Many of the students I took out had never picked up a fishing rod so I had the joyful challenge of teaching fishing to my greenhorns. I typically chose a private lake to take them to —a lake loaded with bass. It took a few hours to teach them basic casting skills but once that was accomplished, they all were catching bass and having fun. I was incredibly passionate about fishing, so my passion transferred to them. It was all about Teaching with Heart.

On the last day before winter break, I would bring several fishing rods and reels to class with me. These were a special type of rod, called "flipping rods." Flipping is a unique way to present a lure to a bass by making an underhanded cast instead of a conventional overhand motion. To understand the mechanics, picture yourself holding a fishing rod with a lure tied to the fishing line. Your goal is to swing the lure at the end of the string in a pendulum fashion and drop it into a specific point in the water just a short distance away, using only an underhand motion. That is a "flip cast." It requires hand-eye coordination and takes practice to master.

I would set up targets on the floor of my chemistry lab—small trays ordinarily used to weigh out chemicals on a balance—and demonstrate the technique. I have spent tens of thousands of hours at this technique so I could flip a lure into a tiny plastic weighing tray on 10 out of 10 attempts. I made it look easy. What my kids didn't know is that I'd won several tournaments thanks to my flipping techniques, bringing home two boats and a great deal of cash as prizes.

Next, I would line up the kids, hand them a flipping rod and let them take a crack. They quickly realized I made it look much easier than it really was. Lots of laughs emanated from the lab on Bass-o-Rama Day, and there were shouts and applause when the rare "flipper" successfully landed the lure in the tray. Winners were rewarded with a fishing lure for their success: some of them mimicked frogs, minnows, crayfish, and other typical bass fare. My students came to love Bass-o-Rama Day just as much as I did!

**Note:** In case you'd like to adapt Chemistry Baseball to your classroom, here are a few guidelines:

-The degree of difficulty related to the question determines the magnitude of the hit—single, double, triple, or home run. I make home run questions brutal and very difficult to answer or solve. Triples are tough, too. Singles are relatively easy to answer, and doubles are slightly more challenging. Home run questions are usually given more time to answer or solve.

-Team members are not permitted to give an answer to a struggling teammate at bat. That said, players not at bat may confer *at a whisper level* with teammates on questions. This promotes cooperative learning.

-There are no strikes, walks or foul balls—the player either answers correctly, and advances, or incorrectly, and is "Out."

-If a question is answered incorrectly the offense goes to the other team. The next batter on the team may opt for a previously missed question or request a fresh question.

-To keep the game moving, allot each team just one out per half-inning.

-Listening is part of the game—if a student does not carefully listen to the question and needs the question repeated, they are out!

-I allow only a minimum base advance on a hit. For example, if Sam is on first base after hitting a single, and teammate Leah follows with a double, then the runners advance to second and third, respectively.

-For any question or problem correctly answered, I may ask the batting student to show the solution on the board or provide an explanation. Again, this facilitates cooperative learning.

-I award bonus points to all members of the winning team, which can be used to bump up their grade at the end of the semester. This serves as great incentive.

-You are the official scorekeeper, so stay on your toes! I suggest keeping an inning bracket off to the side, updating the team scores run by run, inning by inning.

# *STUDENT REFLECTIONS*

*Rena Forester*
*CJHS '10*

While majoring in Special Education at Indiana University, I had a teacher named Jill. Technically, her name was Professor Jill C. Clay, but our classes were small and many of us had her for several different courses, so she asked us to call her by her first name.

Let me take you back to the first class I ever had with Jill. I believe it was Introduction to Special Education. Twenty-two women sat in a large, white-walled classroom. We were arranged in clusters of three or four around the room. After distributing the course syllabus and giving us some time to read through it, Jill flashed her Facebook page on the screen at the front of the room.

As juniors in college, we were shocked -- *"Why is our teacher showing us her Facebook page?"* many of us wondered. (I know because we discussed it afterwards). Jill humbly and graciously went on to explain that it was important to her that we see her as a human, that we know who is in her family and what she likes to do outside of class. By the time we left class that evening, we knew that Jill had been divorced and was now happily re-married, and we knew the names of her four children.

Over the next two years of classes, Jill let her personality shine through in every lesson. She always showed up with a smile, even after a stressful afternoon of carpooling her children around, and she had this incredible ability to find the positive in even the most challenging situations. Jill understood children in a way that not everyone can, with a deep passion for providing each one she encountered with an education that would meet his or her individual needs. Her empathetic approach was contagious. She often tossed crayons and Play-Doh on our tables as we wrapped up note-taking for the period, because she understood and believed in the value of de-stressing and the incredible value of play...for students of all ages.

In turn, her students – my peers and I – were always excited to attend her classes. We'd often arrive early and stay late, to discuss class material, chat about teaching strategies, or just discuss life in general. It was easy to remain engaged, whether we were studying test design or learning about the importance of playing with Play-Doh. Jill inspired us by being authentically Jill, and by sharing her world with us. If there was ever a doubt in my mind about becoming a teacher, simply being surrounded by this woman's vibrant passion for education was enough to keep me going.

Thinking back on it, Jill must have understood that if she was authentic with us, it would make for a safer, more loving learning environment. Students need to feel safe, valued, and cared for in order to take risks. And vulnerability and risk-taking are essential to learning.

During my senior year of university, Jill was diagnosed with pancreatic cancer. She fought hard to keep a positive attitude and make healthy choices for her body. She vulnerably shared with us that she believed the stress that she experienced during her many years working in special education at an under-funded school may have somehow contributed to her diagnosis. Every night, she posted a long paragraph to her Facebook page, always beginning, "Today I'm grateful for God's grace and love...", and concluding with "Today I'm grateful for another day to love and be loved." In the middle, she'd list various additional people, sentiments or events from her day that she was grateful for:

*"Today I'm grateful for...a 1.6 mile walk."*

*"Today I'm grateful that...the boys are having a successful hockey season."*

*"Today I'm grateful for...a shower."*

I looked forward to reading Jill's "Gratefuls" every evening. They not only offered me insight into her state of mind, but they served as an impetus to reflect on my own day.

Seven months after earning my degree, I moved to South Korea to teach English to fourth and fifth grade students. Jill passed away on the same day I landed in South Korea to embark on my first year of teaching. (The synchronicity is so interesting to me.) In my new school, I created a class Gratitude Board with the words, "I'm grateful for..." written at the top, and, "...another day to love and be loved. In loving memory of Jill C. Clay" written at the bottom. I told my students about Jill and explained that the blank space in the middle was for them to write the things, people, and moments for which they were grateful. In a country that places so much pressure on children to succeed academically, the kiddos really took to this opportunity to simply pause and be grateful.

And I'm both proud and thankful to say that, to this day – nearly five years later –I take time every night before bed to list my personal "Gratefuls," in Jill's honor.

*Rena Forester (RYT 200) currently resides on a moshav (a type of cooperative farm) in Israel, where she lives her passion of teaching yoga and mindfulness to children. Before moving to Israel, she spent nearly three years living, working, and traveling throughout Asia, including teaching English to first, fourth, and fifth graders in South Korea and as a third grade teacher in Vietnam. She earned a Bachelor of Science degree in education from Indiana University in Bloomington, Indiana, as well as a TEFL (Teaching English as a Foreign Language) certificate, an RYT 200 (Registered Yoga Teacher,) and two children's yoga certificates from Kidding Around Yoga in Israel and Rainbow Yoga in Greece.*

*Ceylan Bilgin*
*SHS '98*

When I was earning my MBA at the University of Chicago Booth School of Business in 2007, I heard about this amazing economics professor, Professor Richard Thaler, a pioneer in the field of behavioral economics. Everyone raved about his class, Managerial Decision Making. Truth be told, economics was never that exciting for me; up until that point, it hadn't seemed applicable to real life at all. It was all widgets and overly rational thinking. But the buzz about Professor Thaler was so intense that I signed up just to see what all the fuss was about.

Every class with Professor Thaler felt like being at a comedy show, albeit an extremely educational comedy show. He would fill his lectures with anecdotal stories peppered with his humorous delivery. One example was his story about a bowl of cashews at a dinner party he once hosted for his fellow economics students while in graduate school. His guests were devouring the nuts, putting them at risk of not having any room left for dinner, so Professor Thaler took them away to remove the temptation. Upon his return, everyone thanked him for moving the nuts out of sight. But then, being economics students, they immediately launched into a group discussion about the fact that their collective response flew in the face of a standard economic principle that dictates that more choices are better. In this instance, more choices were, in fact, *worse,* and this is one of the stories that helped shaped his initial work in behavioral economics, which examines the effect of human psychology on decision making. It was the only class where I wasn't constantly checking my watch to see how much time was left (apologies to all of my other wonderful teachers and professors). More than two decades have passed, but I still remember this lecture, and many more, which is astounding to me.

One topic that stands out is the effect of *anchoring* in sales and negotiations. An anchoring bias occurs when people rely too heavily on the initial information they receive when making a decision. For instance, if a store is having a sale, they may inflate the original price to make the sale price seem like even more of a deal, influencing your decision to make the purchase. You can anchor the outcome of any negotiation simply by being strategic in how you present your initial case. This bit of knowledge changed the way I write emails, negotiate purchases, and think about human interactions in general.

Managerial Decision Making explored the various biases that we, as decision-makers have – biases that pertain not just to business, but to life in general. Professor Thaler went on to write a *New York Times* bestseller, called *Nudge: Improving Decisions About Health, Wealth, and Happiness*, and won a Nobel Prize in Economics in 2017, so clearly, he had a lot going for him. But humor and storytelling were his superpowers, and he used them to bring his lectures to life.

*Ceylan Bilgin graduated from University of Illinois at Urbana-Champaign with a Bachelor of Science degree in marketing and earned a Master of Business Administration degree from University of Chicago Booth School of Business. She is the Director of Marketing at IET, a refurbished laboratory equipment company in Mundelein, Illinois. Ceylan loves supporting scientists at all stages of their research; is in charge of marketing and business development; and has helped to grow parts sales by 80 percent. She lives in Long Grove, Illinois with her husband, Efe, and two children.*

*Steve Vole*
*SHS '79*

I took an instant liking to Gary Valine, who taught freshman year shop at SHS. As a kid, I'd grown up tinkering with parts, as my father owned a towing company as well as an auto repair with a body shop. So by the time I entered Gary's class, I was really enthusiastic about the automotive field. I was fortunate to have him as a shop teacher for two and a half years; he even made me a teacher's aide for extra credit. At one point, Gary asked me if I would be interested in spending the next few weeks building an engine after school together. Was I ever! We immediately began working on an engine that I learned would be going into a car for the 1979 Daytona 500.

Well, I guess you could say my fuse was lit. After Gary and I tackled that project, I went home to my father's garage and disassembled and rebuilt an engine to put it in my Oldsmobile 442. My father couldn't believe I did it at age 16.

Gary also taught me basic body work and paint. In class, he had a car to use while practicing body panel repair, dent removal, and painting. That sort of intense practical experience helped me win many trophies for paint jobs and restoration work over the years.

Then, after 25 years in the garage repair business, I found myself unemployed. So I began driving trucks from Wisconsin to New York weekly and, within six months, I was promoted to number one driver, the highest paid position, which entails getting my choice of the first loads available as well as the trips I want to take. I'm proud to say I've never had to have my truck towed – a common occurrence when you're putting thousands and thousands of miles on it – thanks to my repair expertise that dates back to Gary's class. I'm the guy who helps our other drivers when they're having mechanical problems.

Gary left SHS in the middle of my junior year to work for a race team. This was also the same time I dropped out and went to work full time at my father's garage. Before Gary left, I shook his hand and thanked him for all he taught me and for being a friend. I will say that I missed him.

*Steve Vole lives in Hebron, Illinois, and works for GBF Trucking, located in Kenosha, Wisconsin. He and his brother also operate Main Street Ice Cream Station in Hebron. Steve's daughter, Mindy, is a school teacher and professional photographer and his son, Steven, is a truck driver and off-road equipment operator.*

# Part III

## *Let them know you believe in them*

*"The dream begins with a teacher who believes in you—
who tugs and pushes and leads you to the next plateau,
sometimes poking you with a sharp stick called truth."*
—Dan Rather

A long with *Mr. Holland's Opus*, another favorite teaching film of mine is the 1988 movie *Stand and Deliver*. Based on a true story, an engineer named Jaime Escalante leaves his profession to try to teach Advanced Placement Calculus to a group of challenging, unmotivated students at Garfield High School in East Los Angeles. After some initial battles with these students, whom have been labeled "losers" and "unteachables" by school administrators, he uses a combination of humor, toughness, and innovative teaching strategies to turn the tide. When all of his students earn impressive grades on the concluding AP Exam, the Educational Testing Service suspects they cheated and forces them all to retake the exam. After the retake, all the students again earn honor grades.

*Stand and Deliver* is a testament to the power of raising expectations, not tempering them, and beautifully exemplifies the very real and powerful effect of letting students know that you believe in them. Mr. Escalante's students had grown accustomed to having the bar set low; he believed in them enough to show them that they could do anything they set their minds to. This principle is an inherent part of Teaching with Heart. Whether they realize it or not, students look to their teachers to serve not just as authority figures, but as role models, advocates, cheerleaders, and even friends. They crave the empowerment and comfort that comes with knowing someone believes in you.

So I never set the bar low for my students, regardless of their grade point average. I believed in each and every one of them, and I let them know it. Then I worked with them to make sure they saw it too.

At the onset of each school year, after I had thoroughly explained to them that I would be setting the bar high for all of them, I asked them the following question: What would they do if they knew I was in the building, but didn't show up for chemistry class? Would one student (or perhaps more than just one) assume the leadership position and take over my role? Was someone strong enough to lead the class through a fruitful activity? Did anyone feel she or he had the authority and commanded enough respect to maintain control? Who could initiate a positive learning experience for all class members?

The first time I tried this challenge, in the mid 1990's, students rose to the occasion. I was moved to tears when I showed up halfway through the class period and the group was functioning exceedingly well without me. There were two leaders at the board explaining to the remainder of the class some of the intricate details of a lab we had just completed. I showered the leaders, as well as the entire class, with praise and accolades for having elevated their own "personal bars" in a way they perhaps had never done before.

My goal was to "fill their buckets" as frequently and as authentically as possible. I wanted them to know I believed in them, in their potential.

Prominent education expert and lecturer Alfie Kohn has authored several books, including: *What to Look for in a Classroom…and Other Essays*; *Schooling Beyond Measure & Other Unorthodox Essays About Education*; and *Beyond Discipline: From Compliance to Community*. In the last one mentioned, which he has described as "a modest attempt to overthrow the entire field of classroom management," [viii] he writes that "children are more likely to be respectful when they feel important adults in their lives respect *them*."[ix] I believe this with all my being. When endeavoring to teach with heart, do whatever you can to convey to your students that you care about them, respect them, and believe in them.

42

# STUDENT REFLECTIONS

*Jan Horvath*
*SHS '76*

From the age of three, I believed I was destined to be a singer. Fortunately, I've had several teachers over the years who have connected with my heart in a way that pushed me towards this goal. The first one who comes to mind is my primary school music teacher, Mrs. Fougnies, who gave me a solo in the spring concert in first grade. My song: *Put on a Happy Face*. Mrs. Fougnies' belief in my abilities, and the experience of being up on stage under the bright lights, singing a whole song as a solo at that tender age, helped set my life trajectory. I remember going home after that concert with the firm belief that yes indeed, I *was* a singer!

A few years later, in sixth grade, Mrs. Fougnies led a production of *Fiddler on the Roof*, casting me in the lead role of Golde. Once again, I was empowered by her belief in me. Being the lead in a musical was a pivotal experience in terms of getting bit by the theater bug, and served as the catalyst for my love of performing. Mrs. Fougnies was also the first person who let me know that yes, grown up people (i.e. actors) do this for a living! Could I possibly do this as my life's work? The seed was planted!

Mr. Urick, the very instigator of this book also had a profound effect on me, through a simple comment he made one day in his class. I was a part of *Freshman Studies*, that giant teaching experiment at our high school that allowed us to trade regular classes like math, history, and biology for "units" based on a common theme, like *"The Family"* and *"Love."*

Mr. Urick, my *Love* teacher, had us present something to the class that we had created based on love. I remember singing an original song, accompanied by my guitar, feeling very vulnerable to be sharing something so personal with my class. When I was finished, it was quiet for a moment until Mr. Urick exclaimed, "Someday, we'll all be listening to Jan sing on Johnny Carson's *Tonight Show*!" What a treasured comment that became for me. It gave me another glimmer of

43

hope…maybe my dreams weren't too far-fetched after all. What validation! What a gift! It still gives me chills when I think about it.

Not all teachers are so supportive. When a student has a dream that's out of the norm, some educators might try to talk them out of it. I remember my high school math teacher begging me not to major in music in college. Once I convinced her that my mind was made up, she said to me, in a very defeated tone, "Well, at least *minor* in math." Although I know her intentions were good – she didn't want me to become a starving artist – her way of viewing my future was so out of line with my own perspective. How much better off the world would be if teachers encouraged students to figure out their passions, then tried to assist them in learning and honing the skills necessary to turn those passionate dreams into realities!

In college, I had the privilege of studying under a handful of mentors who had already logged years on stages which I, at that point, only dreamed of setting foot on. At the University of Illinois, Dodi Protero, a Canadian operatic soprano, was my first private voice teacher. She was tiny in stature but had an explosive amount of energy. She had performed in operas throughout Europe and had played on Broadway in the musical *Oliver!*. Dodi was full of enthusiasm and always treated me with respect and admiration. Ironically enough, eight years later, my first Broadway musical was a revival of *Oliver!* and I felt a sense of a baton being passed on from her to me, teacher to student. She had done it, and now she was helping me learn how to do it too! This is something I have carried on with my voice teaching career – I never dwell on the fact that my age now excludes me from many performing jobs in musical theater. Rather I get excited for my students' successes and try to help them avoid some of the pitfalls, because I've been there and know the territory well.

I ended up transferring to The Cincinnati Conservatory of Music and studied with Nancy Carr, then the head of the voice department. Nancy had enjoyed a storied radio career dating back to the days live radio shows ruled the entertainment scene. She was older and more reserved than Dodi. Nancy, too, treated me with respect and gave me an absolute sense of confidence that I could and would do this work for the rest of my life. Her calm, steady mentorship kept me grounded and gave me a solid foundation for beginning my career in New York City. Like Dodi, she made me feel that I was following in her footsteps. This meant the world to me.

After more than 30 years in the performing arts, I have now dedicated my life to serving as a voice teacher, to pass on what I've learned to the next generation. I want to pay it forward. I now find this role of teacher, to be the true calling of my life.

*Jan Horvath is a veteran of five Broadway shows, including the original Broadway company of* The Phantom of the Opera; *The* Threepenny Opera *starring Sting;* Sweet Charity; *and* Oliver!. *Off Broadway she was featured in Yoko Ono's* New York Rock; *the revised version of* Chess; *and* Jacques Brel. *She portrayed Grizabella in the National Tour of* Cats *and performed in* The Bernstein Mass *at the Vatican in Rome and at Carnegie Hall. As a songwriter, Jan premiered her song "Immigrant's Anthem" with the Cincinnati Pops Orchestra, and composed her solo CD* NEVER TOO LATE. *For the past 12 years, Jan has been teaching private voice, vocal technique classes, and master classes. She lives in New York City with her husband, artist Rino Li Causi.*

*Amy (Nusbaum) Joseph*
*SHS '84*

When I was in the fourth grade, I attended a middle school that was testing out a new, experimental, "open classroom" style of learning. Students were placed into classes according to their skill set for the particular subject. This meant that a math class could have everything from a 9-year-old fourth grader who excelled with numbers to a 14-year-old eighth grader who was a bit behind. There were virtually no walls separating the classrooms, and low bookshelves were the only thing that divided each class.

It was extremely intimidating to be nine years old and in classes with kids who were much older...or to be one of the older students in class surrounded by much younger peers, which was my situation when it came to math. Numbers were always a challenge for me – they still are – so I was already struggling. I also had pretty severe anxiety, which made it difficult for me to focus when attempting to learn a new concept, like long division. To be thrust into this experimental teaching environment made the situation even more difficult.

So, here I was, a fourth-grade student failing math. Because of my anxiety and learning differences, I found myself frozen with fear. (Though it has not officially been diagnosed, I believe I had some form of Auditory Processing Disorder [AUD] as a child. Kids with AUD have difficulty processing, or understanding, what they hear in the same way other children do.)

Then Mrs. Susan L. Schultz entered my life. Mrs. Schultz was an Instructional Aide at our school. She took the time and energy to really connect with me, recognized my challenges, and figured out how I learned most effectively. This was before the days of Individualized Education Programs (IEPs) or 504 plans, tools now used by parents and schools to map out a tailored approach to learning for students who could benefit from additional instruction or attention. Mrs. Schultz understood that children learn in many different ways, and that what is the most successful method for one student may be the polar opposite of what works best for another.

46

I have very specific memories of sitting on the bright orange carpeted floor of the math pod with Mrs. Schultz by my side. She would work through math problems with me, step by step. Up until this point, my irrational fear of math was just one big cloud of dread that prevented me from fully grasping any mathematical concepts. But Mrs. Schultz's warmth and endless patience, combined with her willingness to go out of her way to always smile and say hello to me throughout the day, helped me become comfortable and confident enough to be open to learning long division.

As an adult, I made a very conscious choice to remain in Buffalo Grove, so my son and stepdaughter could benefit from the same wonderful school districts that I did.

Mrs. Schultz never made me feel embarrassed or different (in a bad way) about my challenges. In fact, her approach ultimately helped me reframe my learning problems as learning "dif-abilities."

I've worked as a registered dental hygienist for more than 30 years and patient education is a big part of my job. When it comes to my patients, I have found the most effective way to teach with heart is to begin by truly getting to know my patients and establish a connection. There's almost always *something* I can incorporate into conversation, typically in question/answer form, that provides me with this sort of insight into their personality – I ask about their job, their family, their hobbies. I also ask specific questions to gauge their attitude towards dentistry – are they fearful? Anxious? Or is lying in my chair no big deal to them? Once I have that very important information, I can work effectively and empathetically, which is my take on Teaching with Heart. I have found it's possible to connect with even the most "difficult" patient, once this connection has been made.

I was thrilled to run into Mrs. Schultz at a local store a few years ago, and we have been back in touch ever since! I will be forever grateful to her for taking the time to inspire me to learn, with her compassionate, empathetic, and inspiring teaching style!

*Amy (Nusbaum) Joseph graduated from Southern Illinois University with a bachelor's degree in healthcare management. She is a registered dental hygienist with an associate degree in dental hygiene. She lives with her husband, Steve, and stepdaughter in Buffalo Grove, Illinois; her son is a graduate student and teaching assistant at University of Illinois' Criminology, Law, and Justice degree program.*

*Sarah G. Chiren*
*CJHS '12*

It was the end of our fall semester and finals were approaching when Mr. Urick introduced the concept of radioactive particles to our class. At the time, I had a D average and was far from an ideal student – lazy, apathetic, and more concerned with finding a dress for the Homecoming dance than doing my homework. As Mr. Urick spoke, I was passing notes with my friends.

But my ears perked up when I heard the word *radiation*. When I was much younger, my aunt had been diagnosed with breast cancer, and I quickly remembered that she had undergone radiation, along with chemotherapy and surgery, as treatment.

That day, I raised my hand, and Mr. Urick called on me. I still remember my question—it was slightly off-topic, but was born of a deep curiosity that I had not felt in some time.

"How does radiation both *cause* and *treat* cancer?"

Mr. Urick answered, talking about how DNA disruption can create carcinogenic mutations and about radioactive interruption to the degree that could cause death in cancer cells. After a careful pause, he sat down and told us about his sister, who, at that very time, was undergoing radiation treatments herself.

As someone who had long been perfectly content with a near-failing grade point average, I was surprised by the sense of wonder and catharsis I felt by learning about the details of the treatment. It was a feeling I hadn't experienced in years.

As a younger child, I loved to learn. My dad and I used to turn our kitchen chairs to face the television every Monday night and, at my request, watch medical docuseries together, passing a family-sized bag of Doritos between us. At seven years old, I knew that medicine was my future vocation.

But as a teenager, some combination of rebellion, depressive amotivation, and a profound lack of confidence had essentially erased the goal from my mind. Instead of working towards a future in medicine, I wanted to go shopping and watch movies. I ignored offers for extra help from teachers and used my assignment notebook to create a collage of photographs rather than for its intended purpose.

My life changed that day after chemistry class when Mr. Urick surprised me by calling my name in the hallway outside his classroom. "That was an excellent question," he said, "but this is how you should be every day in class. I know you have it in you."

I reminded him of my D average.

He didn't blink.

"I know you can do it," he continued, "and I think you have a special talent for chemistry. What can I do to help you?"

I had no idea what the answer might be. But I do know that that evening, I went home eager to study for the first time in years. My motivation outweighed my apathy; suddenly, I cared more about solubility calculations than I did about mindless television or about spending the six hours before bedtime chatting with friends on the phone. At the time, I couldn't identify the emotions I was having, but I now know that the fact that my teacher believed in me had flipped a switch in my mind, in my soul. I wanted to study for Mr. Urick, and by extension, for myself. The passion I felt for medicine as a child had been reignited. I saw within myself a future clinician who would one day work with patients and their family members through their most trying challenges.

The following semester, I cried when I learned that I had earned an A in chemistry.

Mr. Urick's confidence in me carried me beyond high school and into my university years. When I withdrew from organic chemistry with a 41 percent average during my sophomore year of college, I heard Mr. Urick reminding me that I had "something special" and retook the

50

class, earning a 98 percent. I'm beyond grateful for that motivation, too; losing my dad to cancer in my early 20s made me realize that my life would be made most meaningful through the pursuit of medicine.

Several other teachers continued to play pivotal roles in my education. In college, my advisor encouraged me to pursue research, teaching positions, and academics far beyond what I believed I was capable of. After completing my undergraduate degree, I worked as a medical scribe in an oncology practice. My physician colleagues have fostered my pursuit of medicine by answering my many questions about diagnostics and treatment protocols, and by sharing their wisdom on everything from the intricacies of appropriate bedside manner to conversations with patients about end-of-life care.

It was Mr. Urick, though, who turned my life around, humanizing chemistry and igniting my eventual path towards a career in medical oncology. He realized the importance of meeting students where they are, even if that happens to be outside the scope of today's lesson plan. He gave me a confidence in myself that hadn't yet been developed, epitomizing the idea that when you teach with heart, you inspire your students to learn with heart.

*Sarah G. Chiren graduated magna cum laude from Lake Forest College in Lake Forest, Illinois, with bachelor's degrees in neuroscience and religious studies, and went on to complete an advanced biology certificate at Northwestern University in 2019. She currently works in an oncology practice in Libertyville, Illinois, helping patients and their families navigate new cancer diagnoses. She is also a religious school teacher. Sarah is beginning a master's program in physician assistant studies in May of 2020 with an ultimate goal of working in medical oncology.*

I was blessed to have many good teachers throughout out the years, but one teacher and one period of time always stands out. The year was 2000 and I was a freshman at SHS in Mr. Kelly's Natural Science class. Instead of a final exam, he assigned us a final project, in which we each had to create a model bridge using nothing but toothpicks and glue. From what I remember, in order to pass the bridge project, the bridge needed to hold X amount of weight.

I was never a straight A student or the smartest kid in class, but I always managed to get by with Bs and Cs. And I actually did enjoy science. Up until this project, though, nothing had ever managed to grab my attention in a meaningful way. But for whatever reason, the bridge assignment got me very excited about school. I remember Mr. Kelly taking notice of all the extra time I was investing in this project – I would come into class early, before school began, and even find a way to get out of study hall to go to the lab and work on my bridge.

Soon, it was time to test out the bridges. But before we did, Mr. Kelly gave out awards for the year. I was not the kind of kid who won awards in school, so when Mr. Kelly announced that he was giving out an award called the MacGyver award, I didn't for a second think that I might be the recipient. The MacGyver award went to the student who most reminded Mr. Kelly of MacGyver, the television character who "had an extraordinary knack for unconventional problem-solving and an extensive bank of scientific knowledge" (according to the show's writers.)

Now, I don't remember word for word what Mr. Kelly said as he handed out the award, but it was something along the lines of, "This award is going to someone who is very smart, creative, and crafty. It's someone who, when he chooses to apply himself, is probably one of the most capable students I've encountered. He could get out of a steel cage with a rubber band and a paperclip." And then he called my name.

I was ecstatic and completely caught by surprise. Up until then, Mr. Kelly had been my favorite teacher and was an adult I really looked up to; someone I wanted to be like when I grew up. Looking back, he was like a mentor to me, though I may not have been able to put that into words at the time. For him to acknowledge me like this at the end of the year is something I'll never forget.

*Jonathan M. Sicora is a co-owner of S.P.E.A.R. Training Center in Vernon Hills, Illinois. He works with athletes from the NFL, NBA, NHL, MLB, Olympics, and World Championships. Jonathan is one of only a handful of trainers globally to reach the Poliquin Level 5 Master Strength Coach, a certification awarded through the National Sport Governing Organization and International Olympic Committee and reserved for coaches who have worked with an athlete who medals in the Olympic Games or World Championships for individual sports, and/or coach an athlete who wins a distinguished award in the professional league team sports. Jonathan earned a Bachelor of Science degree in kinesiology and exercise science from Western Illinois University. He lives in Mundelein, Illinois, with his wife, Jessica.*

*John Beaudry*
*SHS '77*

Science was always a thrilling subject for me. I loved learning about the *whys* of how life worked; about evolution; and how math, geometry, science, and physics dovetailed with one another.

But in 1973, my eighth grade biology teacher, Dr. Shaeffer, made science truly come alive. We were studying evolution. As Dr. Shaeffer spoke, I recalled the story of creation from my catechism classes. These two concepts, evolution and creation, seemed exclusive of one another. Confused, I asked Dr. Shaeffer how the two concepts could coexist. His simple response was a balm to my being: "Maybe God created evolution." He didn't give me an answer; he gave me a possibility, an idea I could expand into.

My early teens were, to say the least, challenging. Like most kids my age, I was searching for where I fit in and what I believed about the world. At some point, my father suddenly and without much explanation told us that we would no longer be attending church, a safe space that had always made me feel comfortable. Now, not only did I feel fractured at school, but my home and religious lives were fractured, too.

I began high school the next year and felt even more out of place. I moved from a junior high of about 100 students to a high school with nearly 1000 students, who seemed to be assigned to groups: geeks, preppies, jocks, burnouts, and dorks. I felt most at home with the group of students known as the burnouts. We smoked pot, dropped speed, and experimented with other drugs.

One day, with no idea what I was getting myself into, I decided to take a hit of LSD, placing the small piece of clear plastic under my tongue on the way to school. Within the hour, I began hallucinating. It felt as if the classroom walls were swirling and caving in, knocking over chairs while everyone else remained oblivious. I swore I could hear the engines of the world churning. The fact that I was high became totally lost on me.

I was a part of the experimental SHS Freshman Studies program. Sitting in Mr. Urick's Self class, we were partaking in a celebration of our special, semester-long projects. The class sat in a circle on the floor, turned off the lights, and lit candles. I stayed seated at my chair, unable to move as my desk seemed to be dissolving beneath my fingers in flaky layers. After class, Mr. Urick approached me, asking if I was okay. I told him that the world was coming to an end. His reply astounded me.

"I know," he answered. "I've been expecting it for a long time." In retrospect, I realize he knew I was high, and was responding to me in a way that he believed might feel soothing and non-threatening. At the time, I knew he was in cahoots with God.

Then he asked if I had taken any drugs. "No," I lied. He asked me how I knew the world was coming to an end. I told him I could hear the engines of the world turning. "Can't you feel the carpet moving?" I asked him. He stayed with me for another hour or two. Then he asked me again, "Are you sure you didn't take something?" Feeling safe and free from any judgement, I said yes and told him what I had taken.

Mr. Urick suggested that I stay after school with him. He would call my parents and tell them that I was staying late to work on a project with him. Then, he promised to bring me home later after the LSD had worn off sufficiently. I shudder to think what might have happened to me if he had not been so compassionate.

So much of my experience in school was of not fitting in, of not belonging. Mr. Urick's care and concern for me—which I interpreted as his believing in me—helped me feel like I *did* belong. The LSD incident was isolated, but his treatment of me was not. He gave his time freely outside of class, when we often continued the philosophical discussions that began in class. He inspired me to think on my own. He clearly loved teaching science and questioned the meaning life as I did. He always met me where I was. Being with him was a respite from what felt like a kind of purgatory to me.

Today, the confluence of the Freshman Studies Program and my one trip on acid still feels like divine synchronicity. That day, under the influence of what I later learned was actually four doses of LSD, I had come to believe that the world was coming to an end, but it also restored my conviction of a power higher than myself. After that I began to read about spirituality and to carve out my identity. At the age of 60, I still get a rush thinking about that experience.

Eleven years later, I would be diagnosed HIV positive. The sense of spirituality I had developed on the heels of that high school experience with LSD prepared me for the death sentence that came with such a diagnosis. It provided me with a fortitude that carried me through one of the most difficult challenges of my life.

Looking back 45 years, I understand that Mr. Urick might have been more afraid than I was. It was risky for him to not turn me in. But he set everything aside to be with me. He allowed me to have my experience. We never spoke about it again. But I always knew he was there for me, cheering me on towards success.

*John Beaudry is a landscape artist and the author of* Garden Sanctuary: Designing for Comfort, Wholeness, and Connection, *a how-to garden design book that takes readers on a transformative journey of creating their own garden sanctuary. He is the president of John Beaudry Landscape Design, dedicated to creating restorative outdoor living spaces and based in La Mesa, California. John's not-for-profit, Community Green, is committed to having every major U.S. city implement green roof infrastructure programs by 2025. John earned his bachelor's degree in horticulture science from the University of Illinois in Champaign-Urbana. He resides in La Mesa, California with his husband, Luís Cerdá, and good friend, Martin Swank, along with their canine companions, Milo and Lila.*

# Part IV

## *Cultivate strong relationships with your students*

More often than not, you could find me chatting with students outside of the classroom. We'd talk in the hallway and, of course, often went fishing together. For a quarter of a century, I sponsored the SHS Ski Club, which involved chaperoning students on Friday night or Saturday ski trips in Wisconsin, as well as leading an annual Spring Break trip to the Colorado Mountains. We would ride the chairlift together, ski the slopes, and relax by the fire afterward with hot cocoa. I also attended many, many school sporting events, starting in my early years at SHS and continuing after my retirement, cheering students on from the sidelines.

Some educators are nervous about revealing too many personal details – or any at all – to their students. They might fear that doing so will blur professional boundaries, or may somehow reduce compliance as students start to see you more as a friend than an authority figure.

But research proves over and over that this simply isn't the case. Students crave authentic relationships with their educators – they make them feel safe, empowered, respected, and seen.
In fact, the building and nurturing of positive student-teacher relationships has been called "the most powerful weapon available to secondary school teachers who want to foster a favorable learning climate."[x]

In an eight-year-long study[xi] of graduate students conducted by Lilian Hill, PhD, an associate professor in the University of Southern Mississippi's College of Education and Psychology, students were asked to name what they considered the top characteristics of effective teachers. Now remember, graduate students have decades of student experience under their belts, and have often already dipped their toes into teaching in some capacity. So they have a lot of knowledge to draw on. As it turns out, qualities that fell under the umbrella of "Relationships with students: Having the best interests of students at heart" were cited equally as often as those in the "Teaching Competence: Knowledge of content and teaching" category.

"Students appear to concur with the literature in adult and higher education that effective teaching involves far more than presenting content and the methods used to convey that content to students," Dr. Hill writes, "Equally important are the affective or emotional processes involved in learning, forming a relationship with students, and caring about students' learning and ability to integrate and apply new information."

There are countless ways to go about doing this.

*-Support them during their extracurricular activities, cheering them on from the sidelines or stands.* Teachers who coach a sport or lead an afterschool club, as I did with the ski club, have an advantage here, as they automatically get to spend hours with some of their students outside of class. Cheering from the stands can have just as significant of an impact. In 2001, my son and I followed the SHS baseball team through their winning of the State Title. Nick, then eight years old, was the unofficial mascot and good luck charm.

*-Share your hobbies and personal passions with them.* For me, it was fishing, but maybe you're a diehard Chicago Cubs fan; go snowboarding every winter; are a skilled baker; love gaming; or have the world's most adorable French bulldog. Share these bits and pieces of your life with your students. Play guitar for them. Show them the scar on your knee that you got from tearing your ACL while playing soccer (or just tripping over a curb) in college. Host a before- or after-school book club for book lovers. Berlin High School social studies teacher and 2012 Connecticut Teacher of the Year David Bosso has told the story of how, when one of his students was having a tough day, he asked if she wanted to learn how to juggle:

*"She looked at me incredulously, and then agreed. Over the next twenty minutes or so, I showed her the movements and patterns involved as she struggled to acquire the skill. I cajoled her, corrected her, and celebrated her. After many attempts, she was juggling! In the ensuing weeks and months, I occasionally asked how her juggling was*

*coming along, but did not give it much more thought. Later that year, she gave a speech to her peers at an assembly and referenced that day. She talked about how I had taken the time to teach her to juggle, and how it was less about the learning process and more about the value of the experience in helping her get through a tough time. Sometimes, the simplest gestures can have the most powerful impact.*"[xii]

*-Eat lunch with them.* If your schedule and school's rules allow for it, join them in the cafeteria and catch up over a sandwich. Or host office hours during your lunch break and invite them to come and hang out. Meals are an easy, low-pressure opportunity to connect, and breaking bread together is known to promote social bonding.

Every week, *The Atlantic* features a conversation between two or more friends in their Friendship Files column. A recent profile[xiii] included a group of four students who became friends with their Bellevue, Washington, high school history teacher, Mike Oliviera (Mr. O, or "O," for short) after joining the school's debate team (he wasn't the debate adviser, but his room was used to host debate meetings, so he was often there, catching up on work.) The girls got to know him a bit and eventually started showing up to his class during lunch. "I think as teenagers, we all complained a lot, and we would always go to O to detail our daily trivial matters, and ask him for advice," Christina said. "O would listen to us, but his very sarcastic humor usually put everything into perspective. He'd be very realistic and make sure that we weren't too caught up in our everyday troubles." Adds Cayla, "I feel like Mr. O was my first adult friend. It's hard to have adult friends when you're a high schooler."

The four students are now college sophomores (at Harvard, Stanford, Brown, and Carnegie Mellon, no less), but the group remains tight, getting together during holidays and school breaks. They even have a closed Facebook group called The Goof Troop (Mr. O's nickname for them), which Jasmine originally created as a way for Mr. O to share pics and videos of his new baby (the young women enjoy watching them for stress relief when studying.)

*-Share your stories with them.* To teach with heart implies letting your students get to know *you* as well as you knowing them. Much of that

59

will happen organically as you share your passions and hobbies with them, but it's also important to tell them stories. They can be funny, poignant, scary, adventuresome, life-altering, tragic... an event that transformed your life or something totally ordinary. For me, this happened in the form of fishing stories, yes, but also when I revealed parts of my life, as I did that day when my student Sarah Chiren asked about cancer and radiation and I told the class about my sister.

# *STUDENT REFLECTIONS*

**Gary Erickson**
**SHS '77**

Growing up, my home life was dysfunctional – I moved eight times and attended six different schools between fourth and twelfth grade, and didn't really have a support system from my family. As a student, I felt like an outsider due my academic struggles, my housing situation (I was living in a trailer in a suburb many miles away from my peers), plus I wasn't involved in school activities due to the fact that I had to work. My dream was to get away from Illinois and go work and live in the glorious mountains of Colorado.

Tom Habley was one of my all-time favorite teachers – and not just because he would stand on his desk and stomp his feet when we weren't paying attention. Mr. Habley must have heard about my issues through the school grapevine because one day, during my senior year, he stopping me in the school hallway and asked about my future plans. I was completely honest and told him. He seemed to understand exactly what I was saying and encouraged me to set a date and make it happen. As someone who felt alone both at home and in school, this gesture made me feel genuinely cared for.

Fueled by his words, I powered through the next four years with this goal in mind and, at age 17, graduated a semester early and moved to Nederland, Colorado, about 18 miles West of Boulder.

There I was, living alone, in a trailer, thrilled to be free but also feeling clueless, nervous, and unsure of my next steps. How was I going to make it on my own with only a basic education? Tom's pep talk motivated me to continue pursuing my dream. He was one of the few adults I truly respected, and one of the only ones to have ever taken the initiative to get to know the real me. He believed in me, which helped me believe in myself.

Back then, I felt that most of my teachers were only there to put in a day's work and had zero interest in getting involved in their students' personal lives. To this day, because of Tom, I feel that when a teacher is able to connect with a student in a one-on-one manner, especially outside of the classroom, it helps build a relationship of respect. That might mean bonding over a common interest or just being there for them. It makes a student try harder. At least, that's what it did for me.

*Gary Erickson has been a self-employed landscaper and handyman for 38 years. He lives in San Diego County with his wife, Rosemary, and two dogs, and is the proud father of three children and eight grandchildren. He currently works four days a week and spends the rest of the time enjoying the great outdoors, classic cars, his grandkids, and crossing things off his bucket list.*

*Carly Silvers*
*CJHS '15*

During my junior year of high school, my family underwent major changes with the adoption of two boys from Ethiopia. I already had three biological brothers, so the addition of two more siblings felt overwhelming, to say the least.

I was going through the college admissions process and ended up leaning heavily on my teachers for recommendations and advice as I began to navigate my future and figure out what it was I wanted from my college experience. At the same time, I knew that at a moment's notice we would be getting the call telling us it was time to fly to Ethiopia to pick up my new brothers. As such, I had to notify my teachers multiple times throughout the year about the possibility of me being suddenly absent.

Most of them had no issue with it. But one teacher in particular was so empathetic and kind regarding the matter that it changed the entire trajectory of my senior year. He was always willing to listen to me if I needed advice, but also remained committed to pushing me to remain my best despite all the tumult. He also told me that he was personally inspired by the adoption my family was pursuing. The combination of these three actions inspired me to be a better student, friend, and sister.

What makes a teacher inspiring is his or her ability to connect with students *beyond* the academic material. Teaching with Heart means knowing your students and holding them to their own unique standard with multiple tailored approaches. I credit this one teacher's commitment and support with helping shape me into the young professional I am today.

*Carly Silvers earned her undergraduate degree in psychology (with a minor in sociology) and master's degree in psychological science from Tulane University in New Orleans. She is currently earning another master's degree, this one in child development, from The Erikson Institute in Chicago. As a Child Life Specialist, she intends to use play as a therapeutic tool for reducing anxiety and stress amongst hospitalized children and their families and to provide emotional and procedural support during the hospital admission process.*

*Greg Wolff*
*SHS '80*

I was a very average student and didn't apply myself to studies like I could or should have in high school. As a result, I didn't connect or spend much time with most of my classroom teachers. Instead, I concentrated on my basketball skills, working as hard as I could to earn a college scholarship.

One teacher who *did* touch my life significantly was Tom Habley. Yes, he taught my physical education class freshman year, but he was also my basketball coach during my sophomore year, which meant we spent many hours a week together outside of class.

When mentoring and motivating us young athletes, Coach Habley used lots of real life comparisons to drive lessons home. He told stories of struggle and commitment, like that of the U.S. Marines training on Parris Island, centering around the hard work required to be a solid teammate. Coach taught us that while sports are a commitment of one's time and energy, it's the sacrifices and working together as a team that breeds success.

We all respected Coach and listened to what he said and I believe we all played harder as a result. I can't say that about the other basketball coaches I've had throughout my basketball career. Coach Habley was a great communicator, passionate about life and coaching. We could feel the love he had for his profession. He had a no-nonsense approach to life. I recall thinking, "He gets it, and he gets us." My favorite saying is, "You're either in or you're in the way," and Coach Habley was forever *IN*.

*Greg Wolf received a full basketball scholarship from Angelo State University in San Angelo, Texas, where he earned his bachelor's degree in marketing. He was an NBA 8th Round Draft Pick for the Houston Rockets in 1984. Greg traded contracts at both the Chicago Board of Trade and Chicago Mercantile Exchange for 14 years. He lives in Cary, Illinois and is self-employed, selling industrial chemicals and commercial roofing solutions. He has two sons who are studying economics and engineering at the University of Illinois-Champaign.*

*Courtney Jane Torchia*
*SHS '98*

Maya Angelou said, "I've learned that people will forget what you said, people will forget what you did, but people will never forget how you made them feel." She may as well have been talking about the special group of teachers who set me on my career path by teaching me with heart.

It was Nate Carter, my third-grade teacher, who made me fall madly in love with science through his joyful classroom (snakes and worms!) and his authentic, ever-present smile. Getting the classroom environment right is so important. Nate had a fun, loving approach, as did Ron Urick, who somehow managed to make even the Periodic Table of Elements cool. Ron put his students before himself – we could tell he couldn't get enough of us. He also helped me navigate a very tricky time in my life, as I struggled with depression in high school. I missed a good amount of class time to attend therapy, and he advocated for me, before depression was considered a disability or something potentially worthy of a 504 plan – or any plan for that matter. Ron was one of the very few teachers who expressed an interest, adapted their curriculum, and worked side-by-side with me so that I could move onto the next grade. It's very unlikely that I would have graduated high school on time without his advocacy.

Another SHS science teacher, Don Carmichael, was always incredibly present and engaging in the classroom, plus he was a regular at so many of our extra-curricular events.

My high school dance instructors, Lucy Vurusic Riner and Angela Cozzi Dauphin,
were more than teachers; they were mentors. We spent many hours together after school at practice and competitions, during which they listened, advised, and laughed with me... they were my life coaches in many ways!

These teachers created environments that made me feel inspired, valued, and safe. Read any leadership book (yes, teachers are leaders!)

and you'll likely see something about the importance of building trust. These people earned my trust and, in doing so, ignited my passion to pursue a degree in science and make a difference in this world, just as they were doing. It's why I chose to pursue a degree in science and enter a field that allows me to care for others.

I recently reconnected with Nate Carter after 30 years. I told him about *Teaching with Heart*. Referring to the principle that helped guide him throughout his education career, he told me, "Students aren't going to care how much you know, until they know how much you care."

*Courtney Jane Torchia earned her undergraduate degrees in microbiology and genetics from Purdue University and currently works as a Quality Manager with global healthcare company Fresenius Kabi. She has spent 19 years working in the pharmaceutical industry. Courtney lives in Chicago.*

**Josh Newlander**
**CJHS '15**

My high school director of college counseling in high school, Rabbi Fliegelman, taught me the importance of staying in touch. Too often, we forget about others to whom we were once close. Rabbi Fliegelman helped me immensely when it came to brainstorming which colleges I wanted to apply to, but our relationship didn't stop with my acceptance letter to Indiana University. He attended school sporting events and showed up for pep rallies. Even after graduating, he'd call us during various Jewish holidays to wish us the best and simply to stay in touch. He helped me learn Torah and gain knowledge on the rabbinic side of my religion, which I never understood before. He cared for me as a student and as an individual, and that translated into me, as a student and an individual, caring about school and my community, respectively. He still reaches out to me on Rosh Hashanah to wish my family and me happiness in the coming year. These are the types of professors you remember, because they helped shape who you are.

*Josh Newlander earned his undergraduate degree in management at Indiana University in Bloomington, Indiana and now works as the director of client relations at a health and wellness media company called* Celebrity Sweat. *He lives in Skokie, Illinois.*

# The day a student saved my life

*"The most powerful agent of growth and transformation is something much more basic than any technique: A change of heart."* —John Welwood

The story that stands out the most features one of my former SHS students in a starring role. It was the Saturday of Labor Day weekend in 1984. Jim Broberg had graduated from SHS four years earlier, but we had kept in close contact and, over those four short years, our relationship evolved from that of student-teacher to that of treasured friendship.

**Jim Broberg:** In the Fall of 1976, I was headed into my freshman year of high school. Before the school year began, we were given the chance to pick our teachers for our classes. With no idea who any of them were, I turned to my two older sisters, Gayle and Kathy, both of whom had graduated and already personally experienced life inside dozens of various teachers' classrooms. I asked them for their top teacher picks. Some of their recommendations were based on teacher personality; others, I must confess, ended up being based on which ones were the easiest. But when I asked my sisters what teacher to pick for my physical science class, both of them immediately said "Ron Urick." Not because he was an easy teacher, but because he was a good teacher.

One time, as I was asking for help with an assignment, I noticed a Bass Pro Shops catalog on Mr. Urick's desk. I asked if he was a fisherman and he said yes. This was the moment our lifelong friendship began.

We began fishing together on weekends, fishing several local lakes. I remember fishing on Sylvan Lake, about 10 miles from school, in early March of my sophomore year. It was freezing cold out but we were both chomping at the bit. After about an hour of casting with nothing to show for it, I was losing faith that anything was going to bite. Ron said he knew there was a big one in there and continued to cast. I could no longer feel my fingers, but Ron refused to quit. All of the sudden, there was a tug on his line and he reeled in a six-pound bass. "I knew there was a good one in there!" he yelled. That's just one example of how Ron taught me to stay focused and never give up – a lesson I used the rest of my life.

**Ron Urick:** *On that Labor Day Saturday of 1984, Jim and I went fishing at a small, local lake not far from his farm outside of Wauconda, Illinois. When we returned to the farm after an awesome day of fishing, Jim invited me to pick some pears in his orchard, which he claimed were exceptional. While we picked pears, I couldn't resist tasting one. But I did so without paying attention, and didn't realize that a yellowjacket wasp had landed on it just seconds before I took my first bite.*

**JB:** Ron bit into the pear and said, "Ow! I think a bee stung me." But we looked at the pear and saw nothing. He seemed fine. A few minutes later, Ron left for home.

**RU:** *I had been stung before without any major issues, so I wasn't terribly worried. I hopped into my car and started driving home. But within a few moments, I glanced in the rearview mirror and saw my face was swelling, with hives emerging all over it. Without thinking, I turned the car around and headed back to the farm. I knew I was going into anaphylactic shock from the sting. There was no time to call 911 – not that we had cell phones back then, anyway.*

**JB:** Five minutes later, Ron was knocking on my door. His face was swollen and he looked like a monster. We got in my Z28 Camaro and started racing down the road. At that time there were not many hospitals around, no cell phones, and no GPS. But I did remember there was a new trauma center in the town I grew up in, Long Grove, which was about nine or 10 miles away. While en route, Ron's face continued to swell even more and he began complaining that his skin was itching from the inside. I could tell he was going downhill fast, and I could tell that he knew it, too. I pressed on the gas and took us to more than 80 miles per hour, taking as many back roads as possible and sliding through a few stop signs and red lights along the way.

**RU:** *By the time we made it to the emergency center, my eyes were completely swollen shut, and I could feel my heart skipping beats. The* *clinic receptionist rapidly triaged me and before we knew it, a nurse was wheeling me down a hallway on a gurney, taking my blood pressure as we flew past other patients and doctors.*

*It was 60/40.*

*To put that in perspective, many hospice centers tell families that when a loved one's blood pressure drops to a number slightly higher than this, that's a signal that death is likely imminent.*

*The doctor retrieved a syringe full of epinephrine and shot it into my arm. Thanks to the miracle of modern medicine, I began to feel better within minutes. My blood pressure slowly rose back up and my heart fluttering ceased. I asked my doctor to level with me – How bad of shape was I in when we had arrived? His immediate response: "You were experiencing extreme anaphylactic shock and were five minutes from coma and possible death. You are extremely fortunate you got here when you did." My former student had just saved my life.*

*-Jim Broberg*
*SHS '80*


*Jim Broberg began working in his family business after graduation and is currently President and co-owner of Du-Bro Products, Inc., which manufactures its own line of products for the radio control hobby industry, the fishing and tackle industry, and the archery industry. It is based in Wauconda, Illinois. Jim has designed hundreds of products, has many U.S. Patents, and was recently inducted into the Academy of Model Aeronautics Hall of Fame. He is most proud of his wife, Marie, and two daughters, whom he loves spending time with in the outdoors...fishing, hunting, camping, riding ATVs, and snowmobiling.*

# Part V

## *The qualities of those who inspire*

*"Life is not about controlling. It is not about getting.*
*It's not about having. It's not about knowing. And it's not even being.*
*Life is eternal, perpetual becoming, or it is nothing.*
*Becoming is not a thing to be known or controlled.*
*It is a magnificent, mysterious odyssey to be experienced."*
—Dee Hock

Closing out the school year in your classroom is as important as starting it. In keeping with the Teaching with Heart theme, how do we "affectively" conclude our school year? On one of the final days of class, I would arrange all the desks in a circle. On each desk, I would have a sheet of paper with something similar to the following typed in the center of it:

**[Student Name]**
**Mr. Urick's Period 3 Accelerated Chemistry Class**
**2001-2002 School Year**

As students entered the room, I would ask them to sit where they found the sheet belonging to them. Once everyone was seated, I gave the following directions: "You have a unique opportunity today to pay a sincere, heartfelt, genuine, but anonymous compliment to each of your classmates. Do not identify yourself after you write each compliment. We will spend the entire period writing, and you will have approximately one-and-a half-minutes for each compliment. When I say 'Pass,' hand the sheet to the person to the right of you. The activity will conclude when you receive your sheet."

This activity was all about sharing our hearts with one another, about letting others know what we found inspiring about them, and always had a profound impact on my students as well as on me. Not only did I have the opportunity to watch my students speak from their hearts, but I also had my own sheet, so I was able to participate in and experience the process first-hand. Students would giggle as they read their sheets, or sat quietly in awe of what had been written about them. And, of

72

course, they would try to determine the author of each compliment. If you decide to adopt this activity in your own classroom, I am confident it will serve as a fitting confirmation of your yearlong goal of teaching with affect and heart—and inspiration. Many of my students still have their sheet from years or even decades ago—it holds its value. I still have mine, too.

## *The qualities that matter*

This final, culminating activity was a chance for my students to view themselves from another person's perspective...a perspective that's usually far less harsh than what we so often use when judging ourselves. When we give others the opportunity to reflect and speak openly, we can gather truly rich data. During the course of researching and writing this book, I decided to apply a similar technique, asking 30+ former students to answer the following three questions:

1. Has a teacher ever connected to your heart (affectively, emotionally, or personally) and changed your life?
2. What qualities of a former teacher or teachers inspired you?
3. How can beginning teachers or teachers in training or be taught to "teach with heart"?

Their responses were thought-provoking and quite moving at times. Many have been woven throughout this book. You will find a comprehensive list of qualities mentioned below.

Authentic

Passionate

Honest

Trusting

Sincere

Fun-loving

73

Genuine

Open

A great listener

Flexible

Takes a personal interest in each student

Refuses to give up on a student

Patient

Kind

Knows how connect with students on a personal level

Willing to share

Willing to take risks

Demonstrates tough love

Is a positive role model

Practices what he or she preaches

Sensitive

Supportive

Nurturing

Injects his or her authentic personality into teaching

Strong storytelling skills

Forgiving

Has high integrity

Creative

Overlooks our shortcomings and guides us to develop our strengths

Develops relationships with students outside of class

Sets the bar high

Non-judgmental

Soulful

Spirited

Loving

Committed

Inspirational

Sees the potential in students and helps them become the best people they can be

# STUDENT REFLECTIONS

**Bonnie Marlewski-Probert**
**SHS '75**

Growing up, my parents owned and operated the only grocery store in our very small Illinois town. They worked from 6:00 am to 10:30 pm most days. Birthdays and holidays in my family were conducted in shifts because the store seemed to always be open – at least that's the way it seemed for my three sisters and me. Time was our family's enemy. With only 24 hours in a day, that left little time for much else. While our parents demonstrated to us the work ethic that the Midwest is famous for, there were many life lessons that fell by the wayside.

Fortunately for me, I had a teacher in my life who filled the gap and forever changed my life's trajectory. That teacher was an English riding instructor named Mr. G.

As a child, I had taken up riding, thanks to a family friend who needed a babysitter for her young son so she could ride her own horses. We negotiated a swap: I would babysit her son while she rode and, occasionally, she would bring a horse over so I could ride in our back garden. I was eight years old when I rode my first horse and was immediately hooked. All the money I earned working in the family grocery store went towards the cost of riding lessons. (In my home, we didn't do weekly "allowances." If you wanted cash, you worked in the store and got paid by the hour.)

Mr. G was a man who understood the nuances of riding so well that he was able to teach the complexities of the sport by using other areas of life as the metaphor. One example had to do with runaways. He taught me that no horse runs off without giving you plenty of notice. They may be small signs, but there will be plenty of them if you pay attention. In the same way, he explained, life gives you plenty of small warning signs that you're heading for trouble in your marriage, job, or health. The trick is to pay attention and make the necessary changes as soon as possible, as you would when riding a horse, before the problem escalates. That said, if you have ignored all the small warning signs – from the horse or from your life – and you find yourself in a frightening runaway situation, he taught me to problem solve with focus and a clear head. "The one who will always be victorious is the one who doesn't give up, doesn't give in, and remains calm throughout," he said. This is the same in life no matter what challenge you are facing. The one who is clear about her or his end goal, focuses on problem solving with a clear head and refuses to throw in the towel will always win.

Lessons like this taught me the power of critical thinking...about higher levels of mathematics...I learned character lessons that included honesty, integrity, leaving things on a good note, elemental training in all areas of life, patience, skill building, team work, and so much more.

The most amazing thing about Mr. G, which I only came to learn years later, was the fact that he was dyslexic and struggled as a child in school because at the time, his teachers didn't understand how to help him. As a result, he had to devise many different methods of learning on his own.

But his own challenge as a student turned out to be his greatest gift as a teacher. Mr. G assumed responsibility for the success of his students. He knew what it was like to have people give up on him and he wasn't going to let that happen to his students. He used to say that it was his job to find a way to communicate with his students so they would understand the concepts he was teaching. No two riding lessons were ever the same because the language he used and the metaphors he relied on varied from student to student. He was patient, humorous, and treated his students with respect, as though we were already Olympians.

The life lessons I learned in the saddle were profound, and I longed to share them with other people. After a decade of Western, English, Dressage, and Jumping riding lessons, and thousands of hours schooling horses from a wide variety of disciplines, I apprenticed as a riding instructor for a year while working in a corporate job during the day. After teaching for a few years at night and on the weekends, I decided it was time to spread my wings and take a risk. In my mid-20s, I resigned from my high-paying, very secure corporate job with a major oil company and bought a horse farm where I spent several years teaching hundreds of students, training more horses than I could count, and focusing all of my efforts on sharing Mr. G's wisdom. My teaching approach mirrored his; I saw it as my responsibility to find a language and metaphors that would allow me to individually connect with my students in a way that would fast-track their safety and their success. And I always strove to ensure that my students were treated with respect.

After running my own barn for several years, I started writing for horse publications because I realized I could reach tens of thousands of horsemen with the stroke of the pen. From there, I branched out to how-to videos, two syndicated columns and multiple book deals, eventually starting my own book publishing house in the early '90s.

77

Most sane people would never attempt this, but thanks to Mr. G, who taught me about elemental training, I approached my writing in the same way that I would approach working with a young horse: one step at a time, one skill set at a time. Today, I'm an award-winning international bestselling author of fiction and non-fiction. I've published the works of hundreds of authors from around the globe and have had the privilege of impacting the lives of hundreds of thousands of people in a positive way. All of that is thanks to one English riding instructor, who treated teaching as a solemn responsibility. I will be forever grateful to him and to other teachers like him, who understand the power of striving to be a great teacher. It made all the difference in the world for this horse-crazy young girl.

*Bonnie Marlewski-Probert is a bestselling author in three countries and the founder of Whitehall Publishing. Bonnie has written more than 18 books, including a series called* Horse Tales for the Soul, *which feature heartwarming, true stories from horse lovers around the world, focusing on the life lessons we learn through the time spent with these magical creatures. She has worked in the horse world for more than 20 years as a teacher, horse trainer, and barn owner.*

*Gary Willmott*
*SHS (attended '76-'79)*

I skipped many of my high school classes, as I felt many of my teachers were just "going through the motions" and failed to show a genuine interest in me. But I was willing to show up for the few teachers who did seem to genuinely care for me and who were passionate about their teaching. If a teacher shared his or her love for the subject and love for students, I was happy to put in the work. Ditto if they talked "to me" and not "at me."

*Gary Willmott is a full-time fishing guide living in Jaco, Costa Rica with his two sons, Matthew and Nicholas. Specializing in fly-fishing, Gary has guided all over the U.S., including Yellowstone National Park; the Tetons; Jackson Hole, Wyoming; the South Fork in Idaho; Alaska and more. He also captains a boat in big salt water tournaments.*

*Joshua Silverman*
*CJHS '14*

After graduating from CJHS, I spent a year studying in Israel with a gap year program called Kivunim. The program entails living in Jerusalem for six months, studying Hebrew, Arabic, and Middle Eastern studies, as well as three months traveling to Jewish communities throughout Europe and North Africa. The entire experience was quite eye-opening to me as an 18-year-old traveling the world. Upon reflection, I realize that it was the teachers who, more than anyone or anything else, really shaped my experience and provided me with the intellectual tools necessary to approach the new experiences and environments into which I'd been immersed.

One teacher who stands out is David Mendelsohn, PhD. David's official role at the time was as a lecturer on topics such as Greek history, the Israeli-Palestinian conflict, and Arabic and Hebrew etymology, but the impact he had on the students was far greater than that of a traditional teacher. I still remember the first time he got up in front of the class and started off with the following words: "You should question everything that I say. Always ask me where I got my information." From the outset, it was very clear that David did not care about grades or percentages; he was exclusively interested in his students learning for the sake of learning. This was a new idea to me, as I'd always been taught that scoring high on tests was of utmost importance. Slowly but surely, David's excitement for learning rubbed off on me and I began to seek out information and ask questions that I otherwise would have either been uninterested in or too afraid to say out loud.

Being around David over the course of the year and seeing how he pursued knowledge with so much joy and persistence, showed me what it truly means to learn.

*Joshua Silverman is a Hebrew- and Arabic-language due diligence researcher at Kroll in Washington, DC. He earned a Bachelor of Arts degree in government and politics from the University of Maryland and, from June 2018 to February 2019, studied Arabic in Morocco as part of the Boren Scholarship.*

*Brad Rubin*
*SHS '97*

High-quality teachers obviously know their content and teach it well. They are prepared, engaging, and often put years of practical experience to work. But highly effective teachers also build relationships with their students and establish a learning atmosphere where it is safe to take risks. Students who know it is a safe place to make mistakes tend to be more engaged and experience the most growth.

Ideally, academic institutions would value this latter set of teaching qualities equally to test scores or data. Schools often place so much robotic emphasis on improving test scores that morale suffers and relationship cultivation takes a back seat. In my humble opinion, the ideal professional learning communities balance standardized test performance with building and nurturing a supportive environment for educators and students alike.

Educators who teach with heart also know there's a difference between *teaching* and *inspiring*. *Teaching* refers primarily to content. *Inspiring* involves awakening something inside someone that had previously been dormant. When a student is inspired, he or she become motivated to do, to become, to change, to grow. Both are extremely important, but teaching content becomes much easier if a student has been inspired. The best teachers provide an almost cyclical supply of inspiration and heart. Some of their students will then internalize this and strive to become the next generation of inspiring teachers. This was certainly the case for me.

I was lucky enough to have a student named Robert as a freshman in my social studies class, then again as a senior in my Advanced Placement (A.P.) government class. The fact that he made it from the first class to the second, though, is a testament to the influence that Ron Urick and other "teaching with heart" teachers had on my own educational style.

During Robert's freshman year, he confided in me that he was "on the brink" of giving up. He was struggling academically and unsure he had what it took to improve. His life at home was also quite difficult; he had recently been involved in a car accident in which his father was tragically killed.

I, along with several fellow teachers, encouraged him to challenge and push himself to keep going. We met with him often, giving him plenty of verbal as well as written encouragement and feedback. We urged him to become the best version of himself he could be, and told him we believed in him. One specific tip I had learned from Ron Urick was that if you take your time, look someone right in the eye, give a strong handshake and speak with conviction, you will make others feel valuable. It helps to foster a genuine connection and often leads to walls coming down, forming the basis for a real conversation and burgeoning, meaningful relationships. I put this into practice with Robert as well.

When this extraordinary young man stepped into my life again three years later, in an A.P. class, no less, I was astounded at his growth as a person and a student. Robert had transformed from a shy and struggling reader and writer to a confident and proficient leader in school. Some highlights from his senior year resume included a 4.395 GPA (top 4 percent of his class); Features Editor and Editor in Chief for the high school newspaper; intern for the *Zion-Benton News*; lead in the school play; and National Honor Society member. He received a nearly-full scholarship to attend Washington and Lee University.

I certainly cannot and do not take all the credit for Robert's growth and achievements. But he later revealed to me that my willingness to spend extra time with him, whether we were problem-solving, working through homework revisions, sharing a pep talk, or simply me showing him I cared about him, made a dramatic difference in helping him ultimately choose a path of grit, determination, hard work, and success. We stay in touch to this day. I have no doubt that this success story may not have happened had I not had the good fortune of studying under Ron and similarly passionate, dedicated teachers, who taught me how to teach, and reach, with heart.

*Brad Rubin is a social science educator at Zion Benton High School in Zion, Illinois, where he has also coached basketball and created the school's Bass Fishing Program. He currently coaches the Bass Fishing Program at Antioch High school (which he also created). Brad earned a bachelor's degree in secondary education from Indiana University and a master's degree in curriculum & instruction from Aurora University. He resides in Antioch, Illinois with his wife, Summer, and two sons.*

**Brendan Snow**
**SHS '03**

Whether it was the high school philosophy teacher who conveyed the richness of Western philosophy and its relentless search for truth…the chemistry teacher who imparted deep life wisdom inspired by Eastern philosophical traditions…the martial arts instructor who conveyed the dignity, respect, and sacredness of Japanese combative traditions (used for defense, not attack)…or the college professor who believed in my capacity to have worthy intellectual insights…my most cherished "teaching with heart" teachers helped me to personally and professionally make sense of the big picture of life. For me, this has meant integrating Eastern and Western philosophical traditions and learning how to be a responsible steward of resources, which ties into my chosen profession of investing.

Every one of these teachers shared an authenticity and willingness to go beyond the material at hand. The key was that they conveyed not just data and information, but wisdom born from direct life experience; some idea or ideas about how to live, how to be good, how to serve, and how to relish life. In a sense, the material itself was secondary; the wisdom, and its conveyance, was the more important lesson, its message about how to live a good and worthy life resonating deeply, long after the material is forgotten. (That said I still remember what titration is and that organic chemistry is damn hard!) Wisdom of this kind, lived and imparted by the teacher, is very hard to come by and is precious.

*Brendan Snow earned a political science degree at the University of Colorado at Boulder. After teaching English in the Republic of Congo for a few months and a stint in Washington, DC, as a finance policy analyst, Brendan earned his master's degree from the Paris Institute of Political Studies in Paris, France. He lives in Colorado with his wife, Puja, where he works as an investment research analyst.*

*Danielle Mall Colan*
*SHS '94*

I loved World Masterpieces and Ms. Maxwell.

Let me rephrase that: I loved World Masterpieces *because of* Ms. Maxwell.

Any teacher who can take century-old pieces of literature and make them relevant to a 16-year-old – make you *want* to read them and discuss them inside and outside of class – is doing something right. I know she was a major influence in my choice to become a high school English teacher, teaching the very same class at the very same school.

In reflection, I've tried to pinpoint what was so magical about that class. Was it just the perfect mix of students? A good time of the day? The literature itself? I'm sure all of those things played some role. But I am certain that Ms. Maxwell was the key ingredient. She brought energy, curiosity, knowledge, and creativity to class every day. I can still remember her laugh, which we heard often, and how she was known for taking in a giant, gasping breath when a student would offer a thought or opinion that she found intriguing, like it was the most brilliant thing she had ever heard. In an adolescent world of peer pressure, competition, and insecurity, when I walked in to Ms. Maxwell's class, I could be me.

A teacher who wants to make a major impact on a student needs to be personable, and they must love what they do. If a teacher gets to know me and makes me part of the class, then I will try to learn anything, even rocket science. And if a teacher loves what they do, that energy is contagious to the students – they can't help but get wrapped up in the lesson, too. It's not about *what* the teacher is teaching that inspires students; it's the way they make you feel when you're in the classroom. That feeling is everything.

*Danielle Mall Colan earned undergraduate degrees in English and Spanish from Davidson College in Davidson, North Carolina, and a master's degree in secondary English education from the University of South Florida. She spent 16 years teaching Communication Arts at*

*SHS. Today, she is the owner of Warrior Wellness Coaching in Grayslake, Illinois, where she partners with athletes to improve life balance and performance. She is also a wellness coach at the College of Lake County in Grayslake, Illinois. Danielle is the 2019 National and World Masters Weightlifting Champion in her age and weight class. She lives in Gurnee, Illinois with her three daughters.*

**Jake Newlander**
**CJHS '13**

Everyone has a special formula when it comes to connecting hearts, and they can all be effective, so long as the teacher is being genuine in his or her approach and communication. As a personal trainer, my goal is to help people become the best version of themselves. This involves connecting with them not just physically, through chest presses and kettlebell swings, but on an emotional, heart-to-heart level.

The ears hear words but the heart can feel emotion. Ron Urick was one of the teachers who instilled this in me. It was actually what he did *beyond* teaching that reached me. He always made sure to ask me how my family was doing, how basketball had been going, how I was feeling about class. His was one of the only classes in which I elected to sit in the front, simply because I felt comfortable being around him. I always knew this teacher would have my back.

Unfortunately, we live in a time right now where the world is filled with so much negativity. Hope and optimism are hard to come by. Students who are fortunate enough to be taught or mentored with heart are in an optimal position to face the world with positivity and gratitude.

*Jake Newlander earned his undergraduate degree in kinesiology from Indiana University, and has continued education certifications in sports medicine and advanced personal training. He is a certified Hollywood physique specialist, a celebrity-based personal trainer, and co-host of the health and wellness TV show* Celebrity Sweat. *Jake lives in Los Angeles but travels frequently as a trainer with the band Def Leppard.*

*Katrine (Lazar) Fleishman*
*SHS '03*

Often when my son claps his hands for another book, I am reminded of Mrs. Zimmerman, my kindergarten teacher, who loved stories in a way that is unparalleled in my experience. To walk into her room was to be enveloped in the world of *Clifford the Big Red Dog*. She inspired her students to love literature, to dive into the worlds found only in books, to discover the lessons those worlds contain. She taught creativity by living creatively. Mrs. Zimmerman made us want to join her inside each book, mingling with the characters, experiencing their lives. When we lived in her world, we learned to think, to problem-solve, to create. The love of stories and words that she inspired in me served me well in all of my years of study and beyond. I hope to pass that inspiration, that legacy, to my son.

So often people forget that when we are operating at our best, we should be a two-way radio, broadcasting and receiving. My mother, my first teacher, often reminds me of that simple truth. The very nature of standing in front of a classroom, lecturing, allows teachers to easily develop the habit of being stuck on broadcast all day. Exceptional teachers remember to flip the switch and receive the transmission as well. When teachers are able to receive, they hear not only what drives their students, but also what inspires them, motivating them to push beyond what they know, to discover what they're capable of achieving. In my 23 years as a student in a classroom, my most remarkable, inspiring teachers have been tied together by their willingness to reach beyond the curriculum, listen to their students' individual needs, meet them where they are, and then challenge them to grow. That, to me, is the essence of Teaching with Heart.

I never had a teacher who chose the profession for the money, or for the cachet, or for the coffee in the teachers' lounge. Every one of them became a teacher because they wanted to make a difference in their students' lives. They entered the game with their hearts. The trick is in continuing to lead with that initial impulse through the day-to-day rigamarole of grading, administrative headaches, teachers' conferences, standardized testing and lesson planning. It's all too easy to lose sight of that original inspiration. New or young teachers need help learning to balance the daily grind with the heart that drew them to the classroom in the first place.

*Katrine (Lazar) Fleishman earned her bachelor's degree in psychology and political science from Wellesley College in Wellesley, Massachusetts; her master's degree in public policy and administration from the London School of Economics and Political Science; and her Juris Doctorate from Georgetown University in Washington, DC. Her work in the Parliament of the United Kingdom, the Scottish Parliament, the United States Senate, and the United States House of Representatives includes education policy crafting and analysis. Katrine now works as an estate planning and real estate attorney. She lives with her husband, Matthew, and son in the Chicagoland area.*

*Dr. Scott Arne*
*SHS '82*

I recall being absent for a chemistry exam in high school. Upon returning to school early the following day, Mr. Urick found me in the hall between classes and asked if I possibly could take the exam at lunch so that he would be able to return the graded tests to the entire class that afternoon.

When I showed up in his class at lunch to take the exam, Mr. Urick quickly explained that he had forgotten he had a teachers' meeting scheduled. Rather than cancel my make-up test, he escorted me to his desk, asked me to place my backpack, which was full of class notes as well as my chemistry textbook, on the floor, and instructed me to complete the exam on my own, leaving it on his desk when finished.

Then he left the room.

With all of the answers at my feet – literally! –  I took the exam unsupervised. I don't think another adult had ever placed so much trust in me, in such a vivid, explicit way. I found myself distracted while taking the exam, as the test questions swirled around in my mind with feelings of pride, honor, and a good amount of nerves. I would have sooner failed that exam than cheated. His trust in me, which was brought to life that day, has been a gift I have carried my whole life.

*Scott A. Arne, DDS, FAGD, earned his Bachelor of Science in biology and his Doctor of Dental Surgery from Loyola University in Chicago. He is the owner and president of the Center for Innovative Dentistry in Deerfield, Illinois.*

*Erin (Stites) Vance*
*SHS '02*

Teachers are sometimes asked to be more than just educators: We're asked to be moms, dads, nurses, therapists, cops, actors…the list goes on. It's not easy, not by any stretch. Teaching with Heart means that you wake up ready to give your students your all, each and every day. Some days that may be harder than others, so you are honest with your students when you are having a low day. Honesty and real-ness pay off in dividends when it comes to fostering relationships with students, no matter what their age. Even preschoolers have compassion when someone is having a tough day or not feeling well.

Sometimes an off day can work in your classroom's favor. Let's say you have a lesson planned, but something unexpected happens that day in the news or at school. The best teachers have the flexibility and willingness to throw out the planned lesson to address a new issue at hand. Or maybe class is going smoothly, but students seem to take a keen interest in something specific that you said. That's your chance to pivot and spend more time on the part of curriculum that connected with the class, rather than power through just so you can check off all your boxes for the day.

My freshman English teacher, Mr. John Kim, knew that most of us didn't want to just read books cover to cover and report on them. So he made a point of leading engaging discussions, connecting the classics to our daily lives. He wanted us to take something away from the literature we were reading and apply it to our current or future lives.

Mr. Kim ended up being my softball coach for three years, so our relationship deepened. We got to enjoy each other's competitiveness and love of athletics. As a coach, he balanced fun with constructive critique to make us a better team. I was a cheerleader in the fall and winter, which often overlapped with softball in the spring. As one of only two softball players who were also school cheerleaders, I often felt looked down upon, skill-wise, as if a cheerleader couldn't possibly be a standout softball player, too. Mr. Kim never treated me that way. He saw my dedication and athleticism, and that was it. To this day, I still play on two softball teams in the spring and summer. My

91

continued love of the sport (and the Chicago Cubs – Go Cubs!) has a lot to do with my time playing under Mr. John Kim.

Anyone going through teacher training can deliver curriculum. But can they connect with students and make the mundane exciting? Those who teach with heart have this quality in spades.

*Erin (Stites) Vance earned her undergraduate degree in fine arts from the University of Illinois in Champaign, Illinois, where she was a member of the inaugural Illini All-Girl competitive cheerleading team, and earned her Masters of Science in Education in curriculum and instruction from Northern Illinois University. She is currently an art educator at Oak Grove School in Libertyville, Illinois, and the head cheerleading coach at Libertyville High School. Erin has coached cheerleading at several schools, including SHS, where, as head coach, she took the varsity team to State in 2011 and 2012. Erin is also the Head Official for the Illinois Recreational Cheerleaders Association. She resides in Lake Zurich, Illinois with her husband, Joseph, two daughters, and two dogs.*

# *More members of the Teaching with Heart team talk about the special qualities that matter most...*

The teachers who have had the greatest impact on my life would have to be my parents! They encouraged me, they gave praise when things went well, they consoled me and helped steer me in the right direction when things didn't go well, and they weren't afraid to let me fail in order to teach me a valuable lesson.

But in the stricter definition of teacher, I'd have to say that I connected with Gary Valine, my high school shop teacher. I loved automotive and mechanical stuff and I believe Gary saw my desire and abilities in automotive technology, assigning me special projects to help develop my skills.

One example: Gary was affiliated with a high performance engine rebuilding company and asked me to handle a precision valve re-seating job on a set of Chevrolet cylinder heads. He taught me how to use the grinding equipment properly and, more importantly, how to reface the valves and valve seats correctly. He was meticulous and demanded perfection – qualities that may have felt burdensome and time-consuming to me as a high school student, but that have served me extraordinarily well as a professional. Math was constantly being snuck into our work together, as well. I ended up learning far more than what was described on the course outline.

Gary recognized that kids come from different social backgrounds...and that's a good thing! The world needs skilled tradesmen and tradeswomen. I believe Gary's motivational skills and ability to teach shop with heart is one of the main reasons why I entered the automotive repair industry shortly after high school.

***Dean R. Solberg, SHS '76.*** *Dean is Director of Engineering at Kold-Ban International in Lake in the Hills, Illinois, and holds six U.S. automotive patents.*

In the first semester of my sophomore year, I had a conflict with my science teacher which led to me making poor academic progress. My mother met with the counselor and dean and asked that I be transferred to another teacher's class, which is how I ended up with Mr. Urick as my physical sciences teacher in 1983.

A few years prior to this, I had lost my grandfather, the man who first introduced me to fishing. Every summer we took a special fishing trip together to Massachusetts, and I looked forward to it all year. When Mr. Urick found out that he and I shared a common interest – fishing – he invited me to go bass fishing with him. After just one day in the boat together, seeing his passion for the art of bass fishing, I was hooked. Thirty-seven years later, I am still an avid bass fisherman.

This teacher not only helped explode my hobby into a lifelong pursuit; he seemed to care about me in a truly sincere way. He used our common interest to get to know me better as an individual, as more than just a student in one of his classes. I thought it pretty cool that a teacher would not only take the time to take a student fishing, but to share his vast knowledge of the sport. Seeing his own passion come alive on the water inspired me both outside the classroom as well as in.

Mr. Urick took me on several more trips over the next few years before my family moved away in the summer of 1984. But we stayed in touch and whenever I came back for summer visits, he always made sure we got together for a day on the water.

*Kevin Breen, SHS (attended '81-'84). Kevin is in retail sales in Temecula, California. He lives there with his wife, Lynn (a teacher!) and they have two children: a daughter in high school who enjoys surfing and a 20-year-old son studying to become a PGA teaching professional.*

A teacher who I connected with emotionally and personally was Mrs. Fischer, my high school algebra teacher and varsity cheerleading coach. Mrs. Fischer always had time to listen to us, possessed an abundance of positivity, and demonstrated a relentless dedication to her job and coaching. She treated her students and cheerleaders with respect and compassion and wanted us to achieve our personal best. Mrs. Fischer had high expectations and taught us the importance of respect, explaining that when we were in uniform, we were a representation of our school. We did our best to make her proud.

I've tried to carry on these qualities by always making time to listen to my employees; holding them to high standards because I know how much they are capable of; giving 110 percent to my job; striving to be respectful of others; and maintaining a positive outlook on life. I also think of her every time I smell Snickerdoodle cookies – she used to surprise us with her homemade specialty at school. The best!

*Kathy (Broberg) Weiland, SHS '76. Kathy studied early childhood/elementary education at Western Michigan University in Kalamazoo, Michigan. After college, she substitute taught for six months before making a career change and entering her family's manufacturing business. She is currently a co-owner of Du-Bro Products, Inc., along with her brother and sister. She lives with her husband, Terry, in Woodstock, Illinois.*

For me, teachers who attempted to connect with me on a personal level have been the most influential. They are the educators who inspired me to access a new part of myself and helped me grow as an individual.

One teacher who I identify as having taught with heart was a landscape architecture professor in college. It was important to him that he shared his love of the subject through connecting closely with his students. In getting to know this teacher and the subject matter, I actually became inspired to pursue personal endeavors which ultimately led me *out* of my landscape architecture major and into nursing, a field that spoke to me more personally. I believe that connecting with this teacher allowed me to access a new part of myself, one that paved the way for an incredibly rewarding career in the helping profession.

***Rose Kiken, CJHS '08.*** *Rose works as a critical care nurse at Legacy Emanuel Medical Center in Portland, Oregon. She earned her Bachelors of Science in Nursing from University of Illinois. She lives in Portland.*

# CONCLUDING THOUGHTS

*"You get the best effort from people
not by lighting a fire beneath them,
but building a fire within."*
—Bob Nelson

How do we inspire? How do we "teach with heart"? Asking these questions is not unlike asking "How does one create a beautiful painting?" There is no one single answer. My hope is that by reading the narratives throughout this book, qualities like passion, energy, intent, empathy, and authenticity will make their way into your own description. Some of my students' stories are complex – some are simple. All are profound and can guide us towards excellence, if we let them.

As I reflect back on those special people who served as my sources of inspiration, one individual truly stands out. His name was Tony B. and he was my CCD (Confraternity of Christian Doctrine) teacher at St. James Parish in Arlington Heights, Illinois. For Catholic students who weren't enrolled in an actual Catholic high school, Sunday CCD classes following church were the norm. Despite my protestations, my parents made sure I showed up every Sunday. I was blessed to have Tony B. as my instructor. He was a very tall, warm-hearted man with a gentle soul and a football player's body. None of us boys were going to try any antics in his class—he looked as if he could crush all the bones in your hand with a firm handshake if he so wanted. Tony was a highly successful railroad box car salesman and held a high leadership position in his corporation. He had a huge family – eight children! – yet still found the time to teach CCD every Sunday. He would often invite all of us adolescent boys into his home for breakfast, where we would sit around his dining room table — a table big enough to easily host a corporate board meeting.

One Sunday, Tony was wearing a gold-plated locomotive tie clasp. I complimented him on it (I believe the very eloquent words I used were, "That's so cool.") Tony took it off his shirt and handed it to me, saying I could have it. I was blown away by his genuine kindness. That, in essence, was Tony: a kind, sharing, most giving soul. I wanted to be like him someday.

The inspiration that bloomed in that moment was profound and left an indelible mark on me. Perhaps "inspiration" is not complex at all — it can simply be an act of genuine love.

The *Teaching with Heart* team hopes that you have discovered some seeds of wisdom in our book. Our hope is that it may serve as a compass that will lead you to inspire students and other loved ones in your life. *Carpe Diem.*

# Acknowledgements

I have countless people to thank for their help with this book. First and foremost are my former students at both SHS and CJHS – you have been a joy to work with and were truly my inspiration. I've always called you, and of all my students, "my kids," because you are not just names on a class list; you have become a part of my heart.

From within that group emerged my Teaching with Heart team, the former students who made this book possible, including those who helped me brainstorm, participated in discussion sessions, and took the time to put pen to paper and contribute their thoughts in writing. A full list of my team can be found on pages 101-102, but I would like to highlight a few here:

Bonnie Marlewski-Probert (SHS '75), a bestselling author and career self-publisher who volunteered to give me direction early on when I didn't have a clue on how to publish a book. (If you ever choose to chase your own dream of publishing a book, I highly recommend her as a guide: info@whitehallpublishing.com)

Profound gratitude goes to Leslie (Goldman) Alter (SHS '94) who Facebook messaged me out of the blue to volunteer her services to be our Teaching with Heart editor. Leslie was my guiding light throughout the writing process, helping to organize all of my former student contributions and to arrange my writing in a way that made sense, while supplementing it with research of her own. Thank you so much, Leslie, for your professional guidance and direction.

Thank you to Danielle Mall Colan (SHS '94) and Katrine (Lazar) Fleishman (SHS '03) who proofread the Teaching with Heart manuscript. Thanks, too, to all of my former teaching colleagues at both SHS and CJHS who inspired me to Teach with Heart.

Thank you to Jim Broberg for saving my life on that fateful Labor Day weekend of 1984.

My gratitude also goes to Tom Koenigsberger, one of my dearest SHS colleagues, who introduced me to many of the quotes featured in the book and offered me some key early impetus to begin my writing. Tom passed away a few years ago and was a deep, spiritual friend and continual source of inspiration.

My most profound thank you goes to my son, Nick, a musician, songwriter, and aspiring artist. Nick, we have walked many trails together. You helped me climb out of a true low spot when I was struggling with my prostate cancer diagnosis in 2018. Thank you for your kind and caring heart. It has been a blessing to have you as a son.

Deep gratitude also goes to my spouse of 36 years, Paula, who has put up with me through the good times and the bad times. Paula, too, was a teacher. We met at a local inter-school meeting in February of 1982 – a meeting I, in truth, didn't want to attend, but was directed to do so by my department chair. So thank you to my Science Department Chair, Carol Graham. And Paula, your heart is full of generosity and compassion, and has been an unending source of strength for our family. Thank you.

# The Teaching with Heart Team

I have had the privilege of teaching more than 4,000 students throughout my career. Each one of them made this book possible. That said, a core team consisting of 34 students helped me take this project from a dream to reality.

Bonnie Marlewski-Probert SHS '75
Kathy (Broberg) Weiland SHS '76
Jan Horvath SHS '76
Dean Solberg SHS '76
John Beaudry SHS '77
Gary Erickson SHS '77
Steve Vole SHS '79
Gary Willmott SHS (attended '76-'79)
Jim Broberg SHS '80
Greg Wolff SHS '80
Dr. Scott Arne SHS '82
Kevin Breen SHS (attended '81-'84)
Amy (Nusbaum) Joseph SHS '84
Ellen Saharack Singer SHS '87
Leslie (Goldman) Alter SHS '94 *Editor
Danielle Mall Colan SHS '94 *Proofreader
Eileen (Li) Rose SHS '96
Todd Katz SHS '97
Brad Rubin SHS '97
Ceylan Bilgin SHS '98
Courtney Jane Torchia SHS '98
Tyler Uteg SHS '02
Erin (Stites) Vance SHS '02
Katrine (Lazar) Fleishman SHS '03 *Proofreader
Jonathan Sicora SHS '03
Brendan Snow SHS '03
Rose Kiken CJHS '08
Rabbi Elli Cohn CJHS '09
Rena Forester CJHS '10
Sarah G. Chiren CJHS '12

Jake Newlander CJHS '13
Joshua Silverman CJHS '14
Josh Newlander CJHS '15
Carly Silvers CJHS '15
Kara J. Fuhlbrugge *Cover Design
Brad Richardson *Videographer

# A little bit about the schools featured in Teaching with Heart

I was blessed with a rich and rewarding career that spanned 43 years, teaching in communities that were passionate about developing high quality educational programs. Both Adlai E. Stevenson High School (referred to as SHS throughout this book) and Chicagoland Jewish High School (CJHS, now known as Rochelle Zell Jewish High School) were committed to developing superior offerings and opportunities for their students.

SHS started in 1965 as a little country school in Prairie View, Illinois, with just a few hundred students. At the time, Prairie View was so obscure that in the late summer of 1965, furniture for the new school was wrongly shipped to Prairie View, Texas. Today, SHS has blossomed into a school of nearly 5,000 students and is one of the top-ranking high schools in the nation, having won numerous awards for excellence in education. In 2019, it received its fifth United States Department of Education National Blue Ribbon School Award (the others were awarded in 1987, 1991, 1998, and 2002). Only five other high schools in the country have achieved this five-ribbon level of recognition. [xiv]

Rochelle Zell Jewish High School is a smaller, though equally rigorous, private school, which began with 26 students taking classes in a rented synagogue in 2001 and has grown to a 180-student school with its own state-of-the-art building in Deerfield, Illinois. It has a stellar reputation for outstanding educational performance, blending science, arts, and humanities with vibrant religious culture and heritage.

[i] Author in conversation with Sarah Cavanaugh, December 9, 2019.

[ii] Judy Willis. *Research-Based Strategies to Ignite Student Learning: Insights from a Neurologist and Classroom Teacher: Insights from a Neurologist and Classroom Teacher*. Association for Supervision and Curriculum Development. Alexandria, VA. 2006. Page 40 of e-book. https://books.google.com/books?id=nw1RBAAAQBAJ&q=reticular#v=snippet&q=reticular&f=false

[iii] *Research-Based Strategies to Ignite Student Learning,* 41 and 43.

[iv] Edutopia.org, "The Neuroscience Behind Stress and Learning," posted July 18, 2014, https://www.edutopia.org/blog/neuroscience-behind-stress-and-learning-judy-willis

[v] Radteach.com, "Cooperative Learning is a Brain Turn-On," accessed December 9, 2019, http://www.radteach.com/page1/page9/page9.html

[vi] HipHopEd.com, "Science Genius," accessed January 2, 2020, https://hiphoped.com/science-genius

[vii] NBCnews.com, "Beats, Rhymes, & Bunsen Burners: Using Hip Hop as Teaching Tool," accessed January 2, 2020, https://www.nbcnews.com/news/nbcblk/beats-rhymes-bunsen-burners-using-hip-hop-teaching-tool-n581646

[viii] AlfieKohn.com, "Books," accessed December 27, 2019, https://www.alfiekohn.org/books/

[ix] Alfie Kohn, *Beyond Discipline: From Compliance to Community* (Alexandria, Virginia: Association for Supervision and Curriculum Development, 2006), p111.

[x] ASCD.org, "Educator's Guide to Preventing and Solving Discipline Problems," accessed December 30, 2019, www.ascd.org/publications/books/105124/chapters/Developing_Positive_Teacher-Student_Relations.aspx

[xi] Lilian Hill, "Graduate Students' Perspectives on Effective Teaching," *Adult Learning*, 25, no. 2 (2014): 57-65. https://pdfs.semanticscholar.org/ae75/d3f6dada0cd6429b4e71477fb07898e1896c.pdf

[xii] EducationWeek.com, "Response: 'Building Relationships With Students Is the Most Important Thing a Teacher Can Do'," accessed December 30, 2019, http://blogs.edweek.org/teachers/classroom_qa_with_larry_ferlazzo/20

18/10/response_building_relationships_with_students_is_the_most_im
portant_thing_a_teacher_can_do.html/

xiii TheAtlantic.com, "THE FRIENDSHIP FILES: When a Teacher
Becomes a Friend," accessed December 21, 2019,
https://www.theatlantic.com/family/archive/2019/02/friendship-files-
when-teacher-becomes-friend/582430/

xiv Stevenson, "Stevenson Earns Fifth Blue Ribbon Schools Award,"
accessed January 13, 2020,
https://www.d125.org/about/news/news-post/~board/district-
news/post/stevenson-earns-fifth-blue-ribbon-schools-award